CAPRICES & AIRS VARIÉS
and
CINQUANTE ÉTUDES

RECENT RESEARCHES IN THE MUSIC OF THE CLASSICAL ERA

Eugene K. Wolf, general editor

A-R Editions, Inc., publishes six quarterly series—

Recent Researches in the Music of the Middle Ages and Early Renaissance,
Margaret Bent, general editor;

Recent Researches in the Music of the Renaissance,
James Haar and Howard Mayer Brown, general editors;

Recent Researches in the Music of the Baroque Era,
Robert L. Marshall, general editor;

Recent Researches in the Music of the Classical Era,
Eugene K. Wolf, general editor;

Recent Researches in the Music of the Nineteenth and Early Twentieth Centuries,
Rufus Hallmark, general editor;

Recent Researches in American Music,
H. Wiley Hitchcock, general editor—

which make public music that is being brought to light
in the course of current musicological research.

Each volume in the *Recent Researches* is devoted
to works by a single composer or to a single genre of composition,
chosen because of its potential interest to scholars and performers,
and prepared for publication according to the standards that govern
the making of all reliable historical editions.

Subscribers to this series, as well as patrons of subscribing institutions,
are invited to apply for information about the "Copyright-Sharing Policy"
of A-R Editions, Inc., under which the contents of this volume
may be reproduced free of charge for study or performance.

Correspondence should be addressed:

A-R EDITIONS, INC.
315 West Gorham Street
Madison, Wisconsin 53703

RECENT RESEARCHES IN THE MUSIC OF THE CLASSICAL ERA • VOLUME XIV

Antonio Bartolomeo Bruni

CAPRICES & AIRS VARIÉS
and
CINQUANTE ÉTUDES

Edited by K Marie Stolba

A-R EDITIONS, INC. • MADISON

To A. T. L.

Copyright © 1982, A-R Editions, Inc.

ISSN 0147-0086

ISBN 0-89579-163-3

Library of Congress Cataloging in Publication Data:
Bruni, Antonio Bartolomeo, 1757-1821.
 [Caprices & airs variés en forme d'étude]
 Caprices & airs variés and Cinquante études.
 (Recent researches in the music of the classical era, ISSN 0147-0086 ; v. 14)
 For violin.
 1. Violin music.   2. Variations (Violin)
3. Violin—Studies and exercises.   I. Stolba, K Marie.
II. Bruni, Antonio Bartolomeo, 1757-1821. Etudes, violin. 1982.   III. Title.   IV. Title: Caprices et airs variés.   V. Series.
M2.R2381   vol. 14   [M41]   82-13793
ISBN 0-89579-163-3

Contents

Preface vii

Caprices & Airs variés en forme d'étude pour un violon seul

No. 1 p. 1	No. 6 p. 5	No. 11 p. 8	No. 16 p. 12	No. 21 p. 15	No. 26 p. 23
No. 2 2	No. 7 6	No. 12 8	No. 17 12	No. 22 16	No. 27 25
No. 3 3	No. 8 6	No. 13 9	No. 18 13	No. 23 18	No. 28 26
No. 4 3	No. 9 6	No. 14 10	No. 19 14	No. 24 20	No. 29 28
No. 5 4	No. 10 8	No. 15 11	No. 20 14	No. 25 22	

Cinquante Études pour le violon formant la 2me partie

No. 1 p. 33	No. 10 p. 50	No. 19 p. 62	No. 28 p. 74	No. 37 p. 91	No. 46 p. 111
No. 2 34	No. 11 51	No. 20 63	No. 29 76	No. 38 93	No. 47 112
No. 3 35	No. 12 52	No. 21 64	No. 30 77	No. 39 97	No. 48 114
No. 4 36	No. 13 54	No. 22 66	No. 31 78	No. 40 98	No. 49 115
No. 5 40	No. 14 55	No. 23 67	No. 32 80	No. 41 99	No. 50 118
No. 6 42	No. 15 57	No. 24 69	No. 33 83	No. 42 102	
No. 7 43	No. 16 58	No. 25 71	No. 34 85	No. 43 105	
No. 8 45	No. 17 59	No. 26 72	No. 35 86	No. 44 106	
No. 9 47	No. 18 60	No. 27 73	No. 36 89	No. 45 110	

Preface

A study of pedagogical violin literature has disclosed that books comprised solely of musical compositions that were clearly designated as études for the violin began to appear around 1787. Because of the absence of publication dates from the editions, it is difficult to determine which book of études was published first. However, Antonio Bartolomeo Bruni's *Caprices & Airs variés en forme d'étude pour un violon seul* seems to have been the first publication for the violin to use the word "étude" in the title and to indicate in print that caprices and airs with variations could be études.[1] Today the name Bruni is heard infrequently in violin teachers' studios, and many violinists are unfamiliar with this man's contributions to violin pedagogy.[2] Fétis was correct when he made the statement: "This musician did not deserve to fall into the oblivion in which he is now plunged."[3]

The Composer and His Works

Antonio Bartolomeo Bruni was born in Cuneo, Italy, in 1751. The boy quickly showed violinistic talent and at about the age of ten was taken to Turin to study with Gaetano Pugnani. Genealogical charts of the Corelli "school" of violin playing include Bruni among the half-dozen most memorable pupils of Pugnani.[4] While in Turin Bartolomeo became interested in light opera (*opéra comique*) and for a time was associated with an Italian opera company. Like other pupils of Pugnani, Bruni gravitated to Paris, where, on several occasions in 1780 and 1781, he is reported to have successfully performed his own concertos at *Concert Spirituel*. No violin concerto by Bruni seems to have survived, however. Bruni elected not to pursue a soloistic career but instead allied himself with *opéra comique*; he was employed as first violinist and later became director of the orchestra of the Comédie-Italienne in Paris.

Bruni was acknowledged to be an excellent violin teacher and was a prolific composer. Between 1782 and 1805 a steady stream of compositions poured from his pen. Extant compositions from those years include the following: eighteen operas; numerous instrumental transcriptions of arias from these operas; a choral *Hymne à la Divinité* written for the 1794 commemorative "Festival to the Supreme Being"; four sets of violin sonatas, one set of six being for unaccompanied violin, and the others being for violin and keyboard; nine books of quartets; five books of trios; twenty-eight sets of duets (some for two violins, some for violin and viola); three books of violin études; and the *Méthode pour violon* (1804). One of the three books of études is the *Caprices & Airs variés en forme d'étude pour un violon seul* included in the present edition. The other two books of études are both entitled *Cinquante Études*: one of these books contains fifty études for unaccompanied violin, and the other has fifty études for solo violin with accompaniment by a second violin. The present edition includes the *Cinquante Études* for unaccompanied violin.

At some time during his stay in Paris, Bruni became a French citizen. In 1794 Citizen Bruni was named to the government *Commission temporaire des Arts*, his specific assignment being "to inventory" musical instruments, books, and music which he regarded as being especially significant and put them on deposit in the Paris Conservatoire for use in public instruction. At that time, in the eyes of the French government the verb "to inventory" meant "to ferret out and appropriate" materials, and Bruni was zealous in this respect. Because of his efforts and integrity, many valuable music manuscripts were preserved during 1794 and 1795. (It should be noted that Bruni refrained from confiscating his own property and that of his close friends and fellow commission members.)

After 1805 came a period of compositional silence, broken near the end of 1815 by publication of a two-act opera, *Le Mariage par commission*, and some transcriptions of arias from it for various instrumental combinations. In 1816 his *Méthode pour l'alto-viola . . . suivis de 25 Etudes* was published.[5] That same year Bruni returned to the city of his birth, where he remained until his death on 6 August 1821. A posthumous special publication of Bruni's *Six Sonates pour le Violon*, "opera 38 e postuma" (originally published as opus 38) and *Six Duos Concertans pour deux Violons* (originally published without opus number) was made in Paris.

Many of Bruni's violin duets are useful pieces for teaching purposes. His violin method sets forth sound pedagogical principles, and his viola method has been republished several times, the latest edition appearing in 1928. That most biographical encyclopedias and dictionaries including accounts of Bruni make no mention of either the *Caprices & Airs variés en forme d'étude* or the two sets of *Cinquante Études* is strange, because these are volumes of considerable importance in the history of violin literature. Even authors of special commemorative biographies[6] have overlooked or have been unaware of the fact that Bruni composed not one, but two volumes of didactic violin literature entitled *Cinquante Études*, both published ca. 1800: one set, designed for two violins, was dedicated to Vanrobais and published by Imbault; the other set, composed *pour un violon seul*, was dedicated to Pignatelli (see Plate I) and published by Sieber *père*.

The Études for Violin

First publication of the *Caprices & Airs variés en forme d'étude* was by Porro and Madame Baillon, "*rue de Petit Reposoir, près de la plâce des Victoires*," Paris, as announced by the *Gazette de France* of 20 February 1787.[7] In March 1787, Bruni collaborated with Cambini, Vanderhagen, and Chapelle in the production of monthly fascicles of an anthology entitled *Recueil d'Airs nouveaux, français et étrangers, ou Journal de violon, flûte, alto et basse*: Nos. 1 and 2 of this *Recueil* consisted of the *Caprices & Airs variés* published previously by Porro and Madame Baillon.[8] In April of the same year these *Caprices & Airs variés* were issued by Imbault, also, and bear his *cotage* 164; this publication was confirmed by the *Calendrier musical universel* of 1788. Imbault continued to publish the *Caprices & Airs variés* until after 1800.

Meanwhile, Bruni composed other caprices, airs with variations, and études for the violin. The Imbault catalog of 1800 lists two works by Bruni—*caprices* [sic] and *50 Etudes*—at the beginning of the column headed *Sonates et Exercices pour le Violin*.[9] According to Wolfgang Matthäus, Imbault announced publication of Bruni's *Cinquante Études* in the *Frankfurter Staats-Ristretto* on 28 May 1799.[10] These *Cinquante Études*, which bear Imbault's plate number 32, were dedicated to Citizen Vanrobais and comprise fifty études for *violino primo* with accompaniment by a second violin. Publication of this same volume of études was announced by Johann André of Offenbach am Main on 28 February 1800.[11] This edition bears André's *Verlagsnummer* 1378.

The 2 *floréal an IX* (22 April 1801) issue of *Affiches, Annonces et Avis Divers* carries *avertissement* of publication of Bruni's *50 Exercices, Suite 2*, by Jean-Georges Sieber, who preferred at that time to be known as "*Sieber père, Editeur de Musique*."[12] Announcement of the publication appeared also in *Frankfurter Staats-Ristretto* on 28 April 1801.[13] It was not until 1806 that Johann André printed an edition of the second volume of *Cinquante Études*, using his *Verlagsnummer* 2228.[14]

Though Sieber's publication is undated, it bears his *cotage* 1542, and the title page (see Plate I) states his address as "*A PARIS* / . . . *rue Honoré la Porte Cochère entre les rues des Vieilles Etuves et d'Orléans, N⁰ 85,*"[15] all of which corroborate 1801 as the year of actual publication.[16] *Cinquante / ÉTUDES / Pour Le Violon / Formant la 2me Partie* was dedicated "*Au Chevalier Pignatelli / Brigadier des Armées de S.M. C le Roy d'Espagne.*"[17] It is this second volume of *Cinquante Études*, études for one violin, unaccompanied, with which the present edition is concerned.

The relationship among the three volumes of violin études is a curious one indeed.[18] It seems odd that Bruni would compose a series of études entitled *Cinquante Études* which contained not fifty but one hundred études, and that the second volume of the series would be written for one unaccompanied violin while the first volume comprised études for one violin with the accompaniment of a second. The matter of different dedicatees for the volumes would not have been unusual in Bruni's time. From the standpoint of the musical compositions themselves, it would be logical to construe *Cinquante Études . . . formant la 2me Partie* as sequel to *Caprices & Airs variés*, especially in the absence of volume one of *Cinquante Études*, because many of the *Cinquante Études* in the Pignatelli set are varied airs and caprices. The purpose underlying Bruni's choice of title may never be discovered; the fact remains, however, that the two volumes bearing the same title (*Cinquante Études*) were published in close proximity, albeit by two different publishers, with two different dedications, and containing differing étude music composed for differing performance media.

Sources

The present edition of *Caprices & Airs variés en forme d'étude* is based on the Imbault publication of 1787, copies of which are presently among the holdings of the Bibliothèque du Conservatoire Royal de Musique in Brussels, Biblioteca nacional in Madrid, Biblioteca del Conservatorio "Giuseppe Verdi" in Milan, and Biblioteca del Conservatorio di Musica S. Pietro a Maiella in Naples. The earlier publication by Baillon was consulted also, courtesy of Bibliothèque nationale, Paris. According to RISM,[19] the Gesellschaft der Musikfreunde in Vienna also owns a copy from the Baillon printing.

The source of the present edition of *Cinquante Études pour le Violin, formant la 2me Partie* is the Paris publication by Sieber *père*, dedicated to Pignatelli and bearing the *cotage* 1542, a worn copy of which is owned by this editor. Lacunae occasioned by some torn pages in the editor's copy were filled by consulting another copy of the Sieber print which is owned by the Music Library, The University of Iowa, Iowa City. Comparison was then made with the copy owned by Bibliothèque nationale, Paris.

In addition, the following music was examined: (1) *36 Études pour le violon . . . cahier I des études*, published at Offenbach by Johann André, and housed at Bibliothèque Cantonale et Universitaire, Lausanne, Switzerland. The title page bears no dedication. This music proved to be a random selection of études from the *violino primo* part of the *Cinquante Études* volume dedicated to Vanrobais, as published by André using *Verlagsnummer* 1378. (2) *Cinquante Études pour le violon*, published by Imbault, using *cotage* 32, housed at Music Library, University of California, Berkeley. This copy consists of *violino primo* music only and bears dedication to C^en Vanrobais. (3) *Cinquante Études pour le violin*, dedicated to Mr Vanrobais, published at Paris by Janet et Cotelle, *cotage* 32, housed at the Music Library, Stanford University, Palo Alto, California, where it was erroneously catalogued (along with some other Bruni works) as "Three piano works." Only the *violino primo* part was available. Janet et Cotelle were successors to Imbault; their publication of the *Cinquante Études* was obviously a printing made from Imbault's original plates.

Examination of the *Cinquante Études* dedicated to Vanrobais revealed that these fifty études are different music from that contained in the volume dedicated to Pignatelli, and that the Pignatelli set could in no way be construed to be the missing *violino secondo* parts to the Vanrobais studies.

The *Cinquante Études* dedicated to Vanrobais are not included in the present edition.

The Music

Cursory examination does not disclose the true worth of the compositions comprising the twenty-nine *Caprices & Airs variés en forme d' étude* and the *Cinquante Études. . .formant la 2me Partie*. These compositions are not exercises but music literature—études whose beauty and value are revealed only through careful consideration of them as "complete compositions with both musical and pedagogic intent and content featuring at least one consistently recurring problem of physiological, technical, or musical difficulty which requires of the player not only mechanical application, but proper study and correct interpretation as well."[20] Careful attention to phrasing is vital. These études were not designed to train the violinist for virtuosic exhibitionism but to enable him to cope with the technical and stylistic requirements of the music of the time and with the structural changes both violin and bow had been undergoing.[21] No charlatanistic tricks are to be found in these études, nor is musicality sacrificed for technique. The technical difficulties incorporated are within the bounds of good taste and exhibit that refinement attributed to the Corellian tradition, since, as a pupil of Pugnani, Bruni stands in direct lineage from Corelli through Somis.

Caprices & Airs variés

The *Caprices & Airs variés* are written in tempi varying from Adagio to Allegro vivace. These compositions cover a range from g to b''' and require use of the unstopped g-string and first through extended seventh position. Twenty of the études are *Caprices*; the other nine (No. 9 and Nos. 22 through 29) are *Airs variés*, each containing three, four, or five variations. Bruni was often accorded praise for penning a beautiful melody—these *Arie con variationi* display the loveliness of his *cantilena*. Moreover, the *Airs variés* exemplify the manner in which variations on an air (aria) were constructed. In Bruni's day the ability to improvise variations upon a theme was esteemed highly.

The fact that specified fingerings are sparse and no prefatory remarks or verbal instructions were printed with the *Caprices & Airs variés* indicates that the études were intended for study with a master. Bruni probably used these études in his own teaching.

The studies are not arranged in progressive order of difficulty. Double-stops are employed in twenty of the twenty-nine études, but triple- and quadruple-stopping is rare. There are many lengthy passages in double-stops, often quite involved, necessitating extended and/or cramped fingerings and difficult and sometimes awkward shifts. Also present are rhythmic intricacies and complicated string-crossings that require dextrous manipulation of both bow and fingers. Bruni seems to favor smaller note-values in these compositions. In single-stopped passages thirty-second-notes are frequently employed and a generous sprinkling of sixty-fourths is found; the double-stops are often written in passages of sixteenth-notes.

No single key tonality seems to have been preferred. Signatures with as many as four sharps or flats are employed. However, twenty-six of the études are in major keys; No. 4 is in C minor, and Nos. 15 and 29 are in F minor.

The baroque binary form (both simple and rounded) is used—only No. 1 is not so patterned, but is treated more freely. Within the binary structure, however, an occasional ternary form (: a : b a :) is found, which would, of course, become a a ba ba when all repeats are observed.

Cinquante Études

Tempo indications in this volume vary from Adagio to Allegro assai; however, some of the studies have no tempo markings, (e.g., No. 10, Polonaise).[22] The gamut has been expanded to cover a range from the unstopped g-string through e'''' (Nos. 16, 41)—an increase of a fourth over the requirements of *Caprices & Airs variés*—which would indicate that by 1799 the violin fingerboard had been elongated to almost its present length. The highest pitches were used not only in cadenzas (Nos. 16, 18), but as a consequence of normal étudinal figuration (Nos. 41, 44).

No prefatory remarks or verbal instructions were printed with the music; however, from time to time a simple direction, such as "*en poussant la première*," appears with a passage. Therefore, like the *Caprices & Airs variés*, this volume was probably intended to be used for study with a master, or by a very advanced student who was capable of interpreting the studies himself.

As was the case in *Caprices & Airs variés*, the *Cinquante Études* are not arranged in progressive order of difficulty; it is probable that key tonality played a part in the way the études were arranged in the volume. Signatures vary from no sharps or flats (both C major and A minor are used) to four flats (both A-flat major and F minor) and five sharps (B major). There is no indication of preference for any one key tonality; Bruni moved regularly from major to minor, or vice versa, for alternating or adjacent sections of an étude (e.g., Nos. 12, 14, 40).

Bruni liberally supplied fingerings for the fifty études, and it was not unusual for him to specify also the string or strings on which a passage was to be played, thus requiring the performer to use the higher positions on all four of the strings (e.g., No. 23) or to play a passage on two strings (e.g., Nos. 14, 41) instead of using only one. Natural harmonics are employed and are indicated in the source by the word "*armonico*" (No. 23) or the abbreviation "*armon:*" (No. 26). The smaller note values, rhythmic intricacies, and complicated string-crossings that characterize the *Caprices & Airs variés* are present to a greater degree in this volume; very wide leaps appear quite often. Double-stops are written in all fifty of the études. Triple-stopping is sometimes employed for an entire passage (No. 13) or for the greater part of a piece (No. 38, Esercizio 3). Only three of the studies (Nos. 5, 10, and 18) contain no multiple-stopping; the final cadence of No. 7 carries the chords into fifth position.

The baroque binary is still the preferred form. However, its usage in this volume is more frequently as an auxiliary to compound ternary structure, such as Minuet-Trio-Minuet da Capo, than as binary, *per se*. At times Bruni used other stylized dances to form this compound ternary structure, such as Allemande and Majeur in No. 25, Polonaise and Minuetto Italiano in No. 10, and Siciliana and Mineur in No. 30, to mention a few. Many styles of music are included in the volume, a fact which confirms the conjecture that Bruni's études were designed to prepare his students to cope with whatever music they might encounter as performers.

Performance Practice

Ornamentation

During the third quarter of the eighteenth century several treatises were written and subsequently published which have come to be regarded as authoritative manuals on proper performance practices to be followed in the interpretation of eighteenth-century music. Among these treatises are the following:

Leopold Mozart, *Versuch einer gründlichen Violinschule*. (1756)

Johann Joachim Quantz, *Versuch einer Anweisung die Flöte traversiere zu spielen*. (1752)

Giuseppe Tartini, *Traité des agréments de la musique*. (1771)

The treatises and the rules contained in them were well known, even in the eighteenth century. Without a doubt, Bartolomeo Bruni was aware of these treatises and the rules contained in them. He applied those principles to the music he composed, performed, or taught. Therefore, Bruni's music should be interpreted according to the rules laid down by the authorities he knew and obeyed.

In the *Caprices & Airs variés* the small notes used for graces appear in values varying from the quarter-note to the sixteenth. In *Cinquante Études* Bruni employed small notes varying from 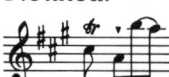 to  ; only in cadenzas do larger note values appear in the very small notation used to indicate ornaments. Infrequently, Bruni marked a slur to connect an ornament to the note it graces; more often he did not do so. Undoubtedly, Bruni presumed that the performer (or his teacher) would be knowledgeable concerning correct performance practices and would supply a slur where it should be applied.

Graces employed in *Caprices & Airs variés* comprise the trill, appoggiatura, and *coulé*. In addition to these types, *Cinquante Études* utilizes the anticipation, *gruppo*, and cadenza-like passages of varying lengths which incorporate many embellishments.

Because correct interpretation of notated ornaments is vital to proper performance of Bruni's compositions, a discussion of these various embellishments follows.

TRILL

Only once in *Caprices & Airs variés*—in No. 28, Var. I, m. 12—is "*tr*" used to indicate a trill; there it denotes a short trill commencing on the upper auxiliary and concluding with a *nachschlag*, or, as Leopold Mozart stated, "All short trills are played with a quick appoggiatura and a turn."[23]

Notated:    Performed:

All other trills in the *Caprices & Airs variés* are designated by the graphic symbol ⁓, denoting that which C. P. E. Bach termed the half-shake, to be performed as follows:

Notated: Performed:

Only in passages performed at very rapid tempo (e.g., Caprice No. 24, Var. IV) is this type of trill interpreted as:

In *Cinquante Études* "*tr*" is used consistently; the graphic symbol never appears. Short trills should be performed in the manner designated above. Presumably, for a long trill the normal eighteenth-century usage would apply, and the *tremblement* would be stopped on the main note slightly before the full time of the note has elapsed (rather than carried to the very end of the indicated time value of the main note) unless the trill was provided with termination. Such terminations were written out by Bruni in small notes, as were any desired ornamental approaches to trills (e.g., No. 18, m. 60, m. 64).

APPOGGIATURA

The appoggiatura appears in both the *Caprices & Airs variés* and the *Cinquante Études*, in various forms: ascending and descending; accented and passing; and, in *Cinquante Études*, measured and unmeasured. Regardless of its classification, "here is now a rule without an exception: The appoggiatura is never separated from its main note, but is taken at all times in the same stroke."[24] So wrote Leopold Mozart, and with this Tartini concurred.[25]

In *Caprices & Airs variés* Bruni's notation of the appoggiatura followed the practice of C. P. E. Bach wherein the very small notation itself indicates the relative length of the appoggiatura. Most frequently the sixteenth-note appoggiatura is used, usually before notes of relatively short duration; the eighth-note appears often; once the quarter-note appears as an appoggiatura before a quarter-note. The slide, or *coulé* (sometimes termed the multiple appoggiatura), is notated in miniature sixteenth-notes beamed together: ♫ .

In *Cinquante Études* Bruni notated the appoggiatura differently. The short or unmeasured appoggiatura is written as a small note with a slash through its stem and flag; here the stress falls on the principal note, and "the short appoggiatura is played as rapidly as possible and is not attacked strongly, but quite softly."[26] According to both Leopold Mozart and Giuseppe Tartini, the long or measured appoggiatura, written as a small note without a slash through its stem, should be "sustained the length of time equivalent to half the note [it embellishes] and is slurred smoothly on to it. What the note loses is given to the appoggiatura."[27] If, however, the main note is dotted, "the grace-note is worth two thirds and the main note the remaining third."[28]

In view of conflicting opinions from writers of accepted treatises, no firm rule can be made as to whether "proper" performance of the passing appoggiatura is on the beat or prior to the beat. C. P. E. Bach insists that appoggiaturas must be on the beat, and it is suggested that the passing appoggiaturas in *Caprices & Airs variés* (Caprice No. 1, mm. 16, 18) be performed in this manner. With regard to those passing appoggiaturas in *Cinquante Études*, the context of the music and the ear of the performer should determine which of the "rules" to follow. According to Quantz, those short appoggiaturas used to fill in descending thirds and transform them into scalar figures "belong in the time of the notes preceding them, and hence must not . . . fall in the time of those that follow them."[29] Concerning the matter of short or descending passing grace-notes, Tartini stated:

> In descending leaps of a third the grace-notes fill in the intervals and form a scale with the main notes. They should pass very lightly and in such a manner that one hears the main notes more strongly. Thus, the accent of the bow or voice should lie much more on the main notes than on the grace-notes.[30]

He stated further that when the small grace-notes are written in values equal to those of the notes they embellish, "the length of the grace-notes is indeterminate; they appear to be worth about half the quavers."[31]

Leopold Mozart, in listing types of short appoggiaturas, concludes:

> (4) and finally, if in an allegro or other playful tempo, notes descend in consecutive degrees or even in thirds, each being preceded by an appoggiatura; . . . the appoggiatura is played quickly in order not to rob the piece of its liveliness by the long-sustained appoggiatura.[32]

Neither Tartini nor Mozart indicates that the short appoggiatura is to derive its temporal value from the note it follows.

ANTICIPATION

In Bruni's music, the anticipation appears as a small note, usually measured, placed either near the barline immediately preceding the note whose pitch it anticipates, or immediately preceding the note whose pitch it anticipates if that note is within a measure. In Bruni's time it was normal for the anticipation to be taken on an up-bow so that the cadence would conclude with a down-bow stroke.

GRUPPO

When Bruni used the *gruppo*, he wrote out the notation for that ornament, using minuscule notation (*Cinquante Études*, Nos. 32, 40).

Bowings

Near the end of the baroque era and during the classical period, both the small stroke or wedge (▼) and the dot (·) were used as bowing indications. Either marking could be used alone or under a slur. In the *Caprices & Airs variés* Bruni employed the dot over notes under a long slur (e.g., in No. 3), thereby signifying that "the notes lying within the slur are to be played in one bow-stroke but must be separated from each other by a slight pressure of the bow."[33] When Bruni used the wedge, he indicated that he desired strongly accented staccato bowing—strokes cleanly separated from one another.[34]

In *Cinquante Études*, the wedge and the dot were still used with the same articulation meanings as in the *Caprices & Airs variés*. There are indications, however, that the meaning of these two markings was changing, because occasionally Bruni wrote the word "staccato" above or below a passage wherein the notes were supplied with dot articulations (e.g., No. 27 Mineur, and No. 36).

The modern symbols ⊓ for down-bow and ∨ for up-bow articulation were not used by Bruni. He employed the French markings: *"ti," "tirant,"* or *"en tirant"* for a down-bow stroke, and *"en poussant," "poussant,"* or *"pous:"* for an up-bow stroke. These directions have been replaced editorially with the modern ⊓ and ∨ symbols.

A marking that might appear at first glance to be an unusual sign occurs in the following example:

Étude No. 50, mm. 63-67

This long, undulating line is merely a slur whose normal contour would have interfered with the low notes printed on the staff above. Such an undulating slur appears in the source for *Cinquante Études*, No. 50, and has been replaced in this edition with the usual long shallow slur. (Actually, the undulating slur may have been an engraver's device rather than a composer's indication.)

It was the custom in the eighteenth century that when several figures of the same kind followed one another, the composer indicated the bowing of only the first of these, marking it with the slurs, staccato marks, etc., which he wished to employ, and leaving the remainder of the figures without articulation markings. The performer was expected to perform the succeeding figures in the same manner as that one which the composer had marked.[35] To assist the performer, in the present edition the word *"simile"* has been editorially supplied; Bruni never used that word in these two volumes.

Editorial Practice

Notation

The notation of note values, rests, and chromatic alterations has been made consistent with twentieth-century practice. The word-order and abbreviations used in indications for *da capo* repeats have been regularized and modernized (e.g., "Siciliana D. C."). Editorial additions or alterations to correct obvious errors, to modernize, or to interpret the notation of the source prints have been placed above or below the staff, or within square brackets, or they have been explained in the Critical Notes. There is one exception to this editorial practice, however, in the matter of fingerings.

Fingerings

In both volumes of this edition, Bruni's fingerings have been retained. (Bruni used the abbreviations "d." or "dgt." to indicate "finger" in the sources.) In the *Caprices & Airs variés* Bruni supplied very few fingerings; therefore, to assure practicality of the present edition, Arabic numerals suggesting additional fingerings have been supplied editorially, and Critical Notes have been used to call attention to those fingerings specified by the composer. On the other hand, in *Cinquante Études* Bruni liberally specified fingerings; editorial suggestions, enclosed within square brackets, are sparse.

Phrasing and Interpretation

Phrasing is inherent in Bruni's notation. Bruni used stem direction in his notation to indicate such compositional elements as polyphonic lines, melody with accompaniment, and proper performance of triple-stops (i.e., whether the pitches in a triple-stop were to be struck simultaneously or broken [not arpeggiated] at a certain place). For this reason, the stem direction and the grouping of notes by bars or beams were not altered editorially, unless by so doing the composer's musical meaning would not be misinterpreted. In this edition the modern symbols ⊓ for down-bow and ∨ for up-bow articulation replace Bruni's *"ti," "tirant," "en tirant," " en poussant," "poussant,"* and *"pous."*

Dots

In *Cinquante Études* the dotting and double-dotting of notes required careful editorial interpretation, because in the last half of the eighteenth century a dot placed after a note, or after another dot, did not always signify that the preceding symbol was to be extended by half its notated time value. In the source, a dot of indeterminate value might be used to indicate extension of a note to supply whatever was necessary to complete an ensuing figure, such as ♩ ♫ being written to indicate ♩. ♬ . In the source a dot indicating extension might be placed immediately after the note to be extended; more often, however, such a dot was positioned at the location of the extension, for example:

Étude No. 2, m. 18

Such dots of extension were used not only within a measure, but were employed instead of the tie to hold a pitch over a barline, or even from line to line.

Octave Transposition

Bruni's use of the Arabic numeral 8 followed by a wavy line 8⁓ to indicate octave transposition of a passage has been replaced with the modern symbol 8- - - ⁊ .

Graces

In both volumes of études Bruni's notation of graces has been retained with one exception: if, in the repetition or recall of a graced passage, a discrepancy occurred which appeared to be an obvious printing or copying error, editorial adjustment was made and explanation given in the Critical Notes. The presence or absence of slurs in Bruni's notation of appoggiaturas and other small-note ornaments has been retained.

Chromatic Alterations (Accidentals)

During the time Bruni was active in Paris, practices with regard to the notation of chromatic alterations underwent transition from those conventions which had been traditional to those customs which are currently in use. This transition may be observed by studying the manner in which Bruni notated his études.

In notating chromatic alterations throughout *Caprices & Airs variés*, Bruni followed an old rule whereby a chromatic alteration does not affect an entire measure but is valid for only the note it immediately precedes except (a) when that same note is repeated immediately, even if such repetition is across a barline; or (b) when the musical figure employing the chromatic alteration is immediately and exactly repeated one or more times, an intervening barline notwithstanding. In other words, when Bruni published this volume the presence of the barline was of no importance where chromatic alterations were concerned. Rarely, a measure occurs in which it appears that the composer either neglected to mark a chromatic alteration or inadvertently permitted an encroachment of the newer practice of entire-measure validity of chromatic alterations. Editorial symbols to clarify the notation or to correct obvious errors have been placed above the staff over the notes affected, with this exception: where the lower note of a double-stop is concerned, the chromatic alteration has been placed below the staff.

In *Cinquante Études*, chromatic alterations in some of the études were notated by Bruni in accordance with the old rule, some études were written in a mixture of the old and the new, and some were notated according to modern practice.

Dynamics

Although in *Caprices & Airs variés* dynamic markings are infrequent, they seem to have been used in a variety of ways. The letters "P" and "F" were used to indicate, respectively, *piano* and *forte*; the graphic symbol for *crescendo* ⎯⎯ appears only once, in No. 26, Var. IV; the symbol for *decrescendo* was not written at all. In Caprice No. 5 the *f* seems to designate an accent on the highest note in the phrase; in Caprice No. 12 the *p* and *f* appear to have been placed to mark the points of lowest and highest volumes in *crescendo* and *diminuendo* rather than to indicate placement of alternate terraced *piano* and *forte*.

In *Cinquante Études*, dynamic markings were used liberally. Dynamic signs have been retained as Bruni wrote them, with the following exceptions: the hollow closed wedge ⎯⎯ (used in No. 50, *Cinquante Études*) has been replaced with the modern *diminuendo* (*decrescendo*) symbol ⎯⎯, and the hollow opening and closing wedge ⎯⎯ employed to represent the *messa di voce* (used in No. 24, *Cinquante Études*) has been replaced with modern *crescendo* and *decrescendo* signs. The manner in which Bruni indicated *crescendo* and *diminuendo* varied. Sometimes he used the abbreviated word "*cres.*" (rendered in this edition as *cresc.*); at other times he wrote out the word. On other occasions, the replacement of *p* and *f* seems to indicate *crescendo* rather than terraced dynamics, and entries in the Critical Notes have been used to call attention to this fact. Most often, however, Bruni used the modern symbols for graduated dynamics: ⎯⎯ ⎯⎯ .

Bruni's use of "P" for *piano*, "F" for *forte*, and "mez F" for *mezzo forte* have been replaced with the modern letter symbols *p*, *f*, and *mf*.

Bruni used no accent markings with notes; instead he seems to have employed "sF" or "FP" or spaced "F F F F" markings for special accentuation. Where Bruni's letter markings seem to indicate such accentuation rather than simple dynamics, this has been suggested by an editorial accent symbol within square brackets above the staff, but Bruni's letter markings have not been removed.

Rhythm

In a few instances, e.g., *Cinquante Études*, No. 2, Bruni's rhythmic intricacies have been interpreted editorially. It is conceivable that in these cases a mathematically correct division of the beat may not have been maintained. The Critical Notes call attention to editorial adjustments.

Critical Notes and Performance Suggestions

The following section documents discrepancies between the primary sources and the present edition. It also makes specific suggestions for solving certain performance problems that arise in this collection of violin études. These performance suggestions are based on the editor's knowledge of Bruni's own notational method and preferences and on late-eighteenth-century treatises on performance practices. In all citations, pitches are designated according to the Helmholtz system, wherein c' = middle c, c'' = the c above middle c, and so forth.

Caprices & Airs variés

No. 1
Mm. 16 and 18, graces in these mm. are measured, and it is suggested that they be performed as even thirty-second-notes, with the graces on the beat but touched on very lightly, in accordance with C. P. E. Bach's preference (*Versuch über die wahre Art das Clavier zu spielen*). M. 31, the grace in this m. is measured.

No. 2
M. 9, after repeat sign, this portion of the measure is as given in the source; temporal problems notationally may be resolved by ignoring this eighth-rest when repeating this section, and by inserting rests of appropriate value in final measures of each section, as necessary.

No. 3
M. 7, notes 8-11 are sixteenth-notes in the source.

No. 4
M. 2, notes 5-7 and 11, the chromatic alterations were suggested editorially because sequential treatment seemed more logical; yet, the possibility of harmonic C minor could not be ruled out.

No. 5
Mm. 7 and 9, notes 7, 13, and 19, source shows the *forte* marking below the three peak notes in each of these mm.; these *f* markings are believed to be intended as accents (see *Dynamics*, above).

No. 9
Menuetto con Variationi—All graces in this movement are measured.

Var. I—Mm. 9 and 10, notes 5 and 9, source shows the *forte* marking below these notes in each of these mm.; these *forte* markings are believed to be intended as accents (see *Dynamics*, above).

Var. II—M. 15, note 1, the grace on this note is a measured one, and the figure should be executed as four equal sixteenth-notes.

Var. IV—Although Bruni did not state a meter signature for this variation, it should be understood to be $\frac{3}{4}$.

No. 12
Mm. 1 and 2, it is believed that these dynamic markings are to apply whenever this two-measure passage recurs within this piece; these dynamics are not intended to be terraced, but are indicative of points of lowest and greatest volume in *crescendo* or *diminuendo*.

No. 13
M. 9, notes 1, 3, and 6 should probably be sharped in view of the stated c'''-natural in m. 10.

No. 14
M. 12, the sixteenth-rest appears immediately before the repeat bar, and the repeat dots are omitted on the right-hand side of the double bar in the source. Mm. 28 and 34, notes 1 and 2 are eighth-notes in the source. M. 36, notes 1 and 2 are eighths, and a sixteenth-rest is inserted after note 3 in the source.

No. 15
M. 26, note 2, in view of the flat-sign preceding note 6, it would appear that the natural preceding note 2 is incorrectly placed in the source. M. 36, eighth-rest is inserted after note 3 in the source; although it is possible that the intended rhythm of this m. was to be two sixteenths, a quarter, and the eighth-rest, Bruni seems to be fairly consistent in using three notes of equal value in his concluding measures.

No. 17
Anacrusis, eighth-rest inserted before note 1 in the source. M. 8, note 1 has no dot in the source.

No. 18
M. 6, grace on note 1 is a measured grace. M. 23, this is Bruni's fingering.

No. 22
Var. II—Mm. 1 and 2, editorial slurred bowing should be maintained throughout this movement in double-stopped passages where one note is sustained against multiple notes in the other part. M. 5, last note, upper voice, this note has no natural sign in the source, but it should be played as e''-natural.

Var. III—Mm. 2 and 7, this is Bruni's fingering. M. 8, this is how the m. is given in the source.

No. 24
Var. III—Mm. 9-17, notes 1, 5, and 9 of each m. are all to be sharped by analogy with the pattern established in m. 9. M. 14, notes 3 and 4 are g'-sharp and a' in the source, changed here by analogy with m. 10.

Var. IV—M. 9, it is effective to slur the last 3 notes of each 4-note group in this passage.

No. 25
Var. III—M. 7, note 10, this is Bruni's fingering.

No. 26
Var. II—M. 5, note 5 of lower voice of double-stop is a quarter-note in the source.

Var. IV—M. 12, eighth-rest inserted at the end of this m. in the source.

No. 27
Var. II—Mm. 11-12, so given in the source; however, stems may have been omitted inadvertently from top notes, i.e., d'' and e''. (See mms. 1 and 2 of Var. II.)

No. 28
Var. II—M. 10, last 2 notes of upper voice of double-stop are eighth-notes in the source.

Var. III—M. 6 to end of movement, fingerings in this section are Bruni's.

No. 29

Var. III—M. 2, notes 9-11, each time this figure was printed in the source, it was given incorrectly as one sixteenth-note followed by two thirty-second-notes.

Var. IV—M. 3, this is Bruni's fingering.

Cinquante Études

No. 1

In this étude, chords notated with stems in two directions indicate where the break in stroking should occur. In a three-note chord, if all three notes are attached to one stem, the chord is a triple-stop with all notes sounding simultaneously. This can be accomplished on a modern violin. M. 23, beat 3, Bruni notated as:

It is changed here by analogy with mm. 27, 61, and 65. M. 28, last note, grace-note notated as a measured grace-note (i.e., without a slash through its stem and flag), but slurred.

No. 2

Bruni used the key signature of three naturals to indicate the key of A minor. Mm. 1 and 5 were notated by Bruni as:

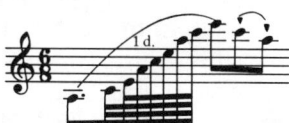

Mm. 28 and 32 were notated by Bruni just as mm. 1 and 5 were, but in m. 28 there was no slur over notes 10 and 11, and in m. 32 there were no slurs whatsoever.

M. 17 appears in original notation as:

M. 19 appears in original notation as:

The first half of m. 33 was notated similarly.

No. 3

Rondo—M. 10, notes with stems downward supply harmony and should be played lightly.

Mineur—In this movement, notation with stems in opposite directions indicates either melody with accompaniment, or polyphony. Where double-stops or chords were intended, Bruni attached the noteheads to a single stem.

Mm. 3 and 4, changes of bow must be made smoothly, almost imperceptibly, in order to provide the sustained harmony indicated by the single note in the lower voice.

No. 4

Adagio—Mm. 3 and 7, the graces in these mm. are measured; Bruni was usually quite careful to differentiate between measured and unmeasured graces. Mm. 6 and 7, the curved line was used frequently by Bruni to indicate *sostenuto* or very *legato* changes of bow; the curved line between mm. 6 and 7 denotes such a *sostenuto*, but the curved line used within m. 7 indicates a slur. Mm. 9-10 and 13-14, the slur from a' to d''-sharp indicates that these two notes are the melody and that the c''' and f' are to provide harmony; in the original notation the c''' was stemmed downward, but its stem did not touch the a', which was also stemmed downward.

Esercizio 2º—The meter signature of the movement is interpreted as $\frac{12}{8}$ as regards the notation; however, the music must be felt in performance as being in 4 with a triplet pattern. In accordance with notational practice common in his day, Bruni wrote each triplet in this Esercizio as being equivalent to three eighth-notes. Even subsidiary triplets were considered as being three eighth-notes. Thus, the composer notated the first triplet pattern in m. 1 as four sixteenth-notes plus one eighth-note, and he intended this temporal sextuplet to equal one eighth-note in a larger triplet pattern equivalent to three eighth-notes. It would seem that Bruni's engraver disagreed with him and originally engaved this sextuplet pattern as four thirty-second-notes plus one sixteenth-note. Many white blotches in the source reveal that a correction was made, and the engraving was restored to that in Bruni's manuscript: four sixteenth-notes plus one eighth-note, followed by an eighth-rest and an eighth-note to constitute the first main triplet within the measure. This pattern was used again for the third main triplet in the measure.

Mm. 1-4, the first section of this binary form contains only half as many mm. as the other étude-variations in this study; however, no repeat of the section was intended, since m. 4 is complete. M. 16, final rest is a half-rest in the source.

Esercizio 3º—M. 7, last 2 beats-m. 8, first 2 beats, comparison of this octavo passage with that in mm. 14-16 seems to indicate the omission of one m. from the first passage; on the other hand Bruni has employed the correct number of mm. in the first section of this étude-variation just as it is.

Esercizio 5º—M. 9, notes 1 and 2 of lower voice of double-stop, the curved line connecting these pitches is not a tie; rather, it denotes a very smooth change of bow.

Esercizio 6º—M. 16, note 7, and m. 23, note 8, even though it is an eighth-note, this note must be played as half of a beat; therefore it must be of longer duration than the previous triplet eighths.

No. 6
Tempo di Minuetto—M. 1, this m. sets the bowing pattern that should be followed for these figures throughout the section. M. 9, this m. sets the bowing pattern that should be followed for these figures throughout the section.

Mineur—Throughout this movement, the *f* or "forte" marking seems to indicate an accent rather than a dynamic.

No. 7
Aria—M. 3, play graces measured, as four equal sixty-fourth-notes, but play the first two of them lightly. Mm. 5 and 6, after establishing a pattern by writing out the notation of this figure in the first two mm., Bruni employed the indeterminate-valued dot in succeeding mm., and the performer was expected to apply correct time values; here his notation was as follows:

Thus, the first dot is normal (i.e., half the value of the note it follows), but the second dot assumes the value necessary to complete the figure, which in this case is a thirty-second-note. M. 11, in the source note 1 (triple-stop) is double-dotted, which was inconsistent with the pattern in m. 3. M. 13, note 1 (triple-stop) was not double-dotted here, but the figure was written out to indicate that only the c''' was to be held over. M. 30, notes 10-12, editorial slur suggested here in order that the movement may end with down-bow; Bruni may have wanted an up-bow ending.

Allemande—The meter signature printed in the source is $\frac{3}{4}$, but notation is given for $\frac{3}{8}$ meter.

No. 8
Esercizio—M. 10, note 10 is b''' in the source, which does not conform to the established melodic pattern; it would appear that g''' was intended.

Minuetto—Mm. 6, 8, and 17, in these and similar mm. of this section, Bruni's probable intention was that the longer slur should prevail and that the polyphony of the other part should be articulated without disrupting continuity of this longer slur.

Majeur—M. 12, note 1 is a quarter-note in the source, resulting in too many counts for this m.; changed here by analogy with similar figure in m. 20. M. 14, note 5 is c'' in the source; changed here by analogy with scalar pattern in mm. 21-22.

No. 9
Andante sostenuto—M. 9, note 1, in the source the lower voice of double-stop is an eighth-note (e''-flat), which would be dissonant with the e''-natural of note 3; changed here by analogy with similar figure in m. 10.

Esercizio 2º—Mm. 1-4, the old custom of using a dot after the barline instead of a note to indicate a pitch tied across that barline becomes problematic when such a dot is misplaced; original notation for the opening of this movement is:

The dots are in proper position commencing with m. 5 of the source, however; bowing articulation was determined by Bruni's placement of a slur over dotted note within the m. and carrying slightly over into next pitch. M. 11, this m. was short a quarter-beat because of the omission of the dot (rendered here as a tied sixteenth-note) after the f'' in the original.

No. 10
Polonaise—M. 2, intended bowing for this figure is enigmatic; it appeared in three different manners in the source. M. 30, notes 2 and 3 are sixteenth-notes in the source.

Majeur—Mm. 3 and 5-7, notation in these mm. indicates Bruni's interpretation of this figure; this interpretation should be applied to mm. 11 and 13-15, and others of a similar nature. Mm. 25-28, note Bruni's deliberate phrasing in the notation of these mm.

No. 11
Allegretto con moto—It is presumed that Bruni intended to use the words "con moto," but whenever the phrase appears in the source, the printing reads "con molto." Mm. 1 ff., presumably, Bruni intended each double-stop occurring on the first beat of a m. to be *forte*. M. 22, note 2, lower voice of double-stop, in performance this dotted note should be broken into 3 eighth-notes. Mm. 65-72, the polyphony in this section should be clearly delineated.

No. 12
Mineur—Mm. 17 ff., while it is conceivable that Bruni meant this *bariolage* passage to be slurred by twos, it seems more probable that he intended separate bows for contrast.

No. 14
Tempo di Minuetto—M. 21, last rest is a sixteenth-rest in the source, thus causing this m. to be short by one-fourth of a beat.

Mineur—M. 13, Bruni's specified bowings do not seem to create the effect called for by his words "*en poussant la première*" ("first note of m. [or figures] in up-bow"). The editorial slur placed over the first two notes of the first triplet figure will cause each m. to commence with an up-bow, but it will also cause the passage to conclude with an up-bow—which may have been what Bruni intended. M. 27, beat 3, the grace-note is e''-flat in the source; it should probably be d'.

No. 16
Introduzione—M. 25, original notation of the third figure after the first fermata is:

No. 17
Tempo di Minuetto—M. 2, note 4 has a fingering indication "1" in the source, which is obviously a misprint.

Mineur—M. 15, notes 1 and 2 of lower voice of double-stop are dotted eighth and sixteenth. The variable-value dot is employed in m. 15, and the sixteenth-note should be played as a triplet-eighth-note; hence the editorial notation.

No. 18
Allegro moderato—M. 22, Bruni may have intended to use a C-natural throughout the scale-passage in this m.; however, it seems more logical to treat it as a D-major scale. And since all of the other *roulades* are notated to be articulated in 2 bow strokes, this should conform. M. 63, note 2 of lower voice of double-stop, possibly this note should be c', if Bruni intended musical cadence rhyme.

No. 19
Preludio—M. 4, note 3 is c'' in the source; changed here by analogy with prevailing melodic pattern.

Allegretto—M. 10, last note-m. 11, note 1, editorial slur added here by analogy with mm. 14-15. M. 24, note 1 of lower voice of double-stop is b' in the source; changed here by analogy with the pattern of a seventh occurring on the first beat of mm. 22 and 23. M. 26, in source, note 1 (triple-stop) is dotted, and note 2 (triple-stop) and ties do not occur. M. 43, this is one of several instances where the number of beats in anacrusis and final measure do not total to match the meter signature.

No. 21
This piece is not numbered in the source, but it is indented and headed as the other études are.

Allegro—M. 1, note 1, the *forte* marking seems to indicate an accent on the first note in each group of 4 sixteenths.

No. 22
Plus animé—M. 8b, source shows an opening repeat sign before the anacrusis commencing the second section of this binary form; this repeat barline is probably a printing error inasmuch as the second section of the binary form concludes with an Adagio and is not repeated; instead, the music proceeds directly to the first section of the binary form, which is written out in lieu of a *da capo*.

No. 23
Andante moderato—Mm. 9-14, and m. 34, play as:

Mm. 38-39, this passage seems to read better without the slur that connects these mm.; the slur is not used when this music is repeated in mm. 41-42. M. 60, note 3 of upper voice of double-stop, although Bruni's specified fingering for this note is 2, this may have been a printing error, since it does not agree with the previously used fingering pattern. M. 80, in the source, the printing of the beam of the 3 eighth-notes may have obliterated the dot for extension of the d'' pitch. For comparison, original notation of m. 25 is given here also:

No. 25
Majeur—Mm. 7-10 and 29-32, in these mm., changes of bow should be made as smoothly as possible so as to be imperceptible.

No. 27
Pastorale—M. 8, note 1 of lower voice of double-stop, notation given as in the source; no second dot appears to indicate extension of the d'' pitch for the length of the slur, though musicality seems to indicate that such extension should occur.

Mineur—M. 5, here Bruni is using the dot above the note to indicate staccato, but he uses the word "staccato" also; more frequently Bruni followed the older notational method of using the wedge to indicate staccato bowing.

No. 28
Esercizio 2º—Source heading is "Con più Molto."
Esercizio 4º—M. 3, note 2 of lower voice is an eighth-note. M. 9, see m. 13 for the way in which the grace-notes are to be performed.
Esercizio 5º—M. 1, note 1 has *p* dynamic marking in the source; changed here by analogy with the dynamics pattern in the remainder of the movement.

No. 30
Siciliana—Source spells the title "Sicilliana," and at the end of the Mineur section it gives the indication "Sicilliano D.C." M. 4, beat 6, the down-bow indicated here may have been a misprint in the source, in

view of the lack of a similar marking on beat 6 of m. 22. M. 24, stems in different directions indicate where these chords are to be broken in stroking.

Mineur—Mm. 5 ff., Bruni's requested phrasing should be noted in such passages.

No. 31

Tempo di Minuetto—M. 7, note 6 of lower voice of double-stop, although Bruni has indicated first finger for this note, a b'-natural rather than a b'-flat is written in the source, and a second finger would have to be used.

Mineur—M. 30 appears here just as it is given in the source; however, it is possible that a misprint occurred and that m. 30 should be identical with m. 4. M. 44, m. comprised of quarter-note and two quarter-rests in the source; as stated above, Bruni's concluding m. sometimes does not reflect his borrowings for anacrusis.

No. 32

Aria—Mm. 5-7, this passage should be played smoothly with changes of bow that are imperceptible.

No. 33

Tempo di Minuetto—Anacrusis, note 2 (double-stop) is an eighth-note in the source. Mm. 17 ff., this passage must be very sustained, with smooth changes of bow; the chain of slurs in the lower voice is Bruni's way of notating *sostenuto*.

Mineur—M. 3, stems in different directions indicate where the break should occur in stroking the bow.

No. 35

Andante—Source heading is "Andante con Molto."

Esercizio 2º—Mm. 1, 3, 5, 23, 25, and 27, notes 10-12, this figure is to be interpreted as a triplet, with the dotted note being the equivalent of 2 triplet-sixteenth-notes. M. 33, notes 2 and 4, trills are so notated in the source; possibly Bruni intended that the trill be on the c'' rather than on the f''.

Esercizio 3º—M. 11, note 4 and note 5 (double-stop) are thirty-second-notes, note 6 (double-stop) is a sixteenth-note, and rest 2 is a sixteenth-rest in the source. M. 32, note 1 (double-stop) is a sixteenth-note, which places too many counts in the measure.

No. 36

Introduzione—M. 4, note 3, lower voice of double-stop is b-flat in the source.

Allegro moderato—M. 42, note 4 (double-stop) is an eighth-note, and the fermata is placed over the eighth-rest in the source.

No. 37

Tempo di Minuetto—M. 25, note 1, source gives eighth-rest in lower voice. M. 26, note 1, lower voice of double-stop is notated as in the source.

No. 38

Aria—M. 12, note 2 of lower voice is a quarter-note in the source.

Esercizio 4º—M. 10, rest 1 is a quarter-rest in the source. M. 11, note 8 is e''-flat in source.

No. 39

Allegro—Notation of first measure indicates phrasing to be followed throughout.

No. 40

Allegro—Source shows three flats in printed key signature, but a former owner apparently believed this to be in error and had inked in a D-flat in the signature on all staves in the minor portion; copy at The University of Iowa shows same alteration made. However, after considerable deliberation, this editor is inclined to let the three-flat signature stand.

No. 41

Esercizio—M. 1, notation of first m. indicates phrasing to be followed. Mm. 22 ff., the performer should continue phrasing by two throughout the passage. Mm. 35-36, in this étude Bruni sometimes used a pair of diagonal slashes to indicate the repetition of a group of four sixteenth-notes, and mm. 35-36 are the first places in the source where such slashes are used; in m. 35 diagonal slashes replace notes 5-8 and 13-16, and in m. 36 diagonal slashes replace notes 5-16. M. 53, the repeat marking here presumably indicates that only the previous Allegro section is to be repeated, but in view of the fact that the separate sections of this étude are not indented as movements, it is quite possible that the composer meant for the entire 53 mm. to serve as the first half of a binary form and that this is what is to be repeated. Note that Bruni did not use the repeat symbol at the commencement of m. 54 but did indicate in m. 136 that this section was to be repeated.

No. 43

Tempo di Minuetto—M. 9 and throughout the movement, the graces are measured.

No. 44

Andante—M. 2, note 1 has dot above it, note 7 is a dotted eighth, note 8 and tie do not occur, note 14 is a dotted eighth, and note 15 and tie do not occur in the source. M. 47, see entry for m. 2. M. 99, last 6 notes are all sixteenth-notes in the source.

No. 46

Allegretto—M. 25, note 1 is d''' in the source.

Grazioso—M. 36, note 1, lower voice of double-stop is a quarter-note in the source.

No. 47

Moderato—Anacrusis, these two eighth-notes are part of a triplet figure, as revealed by the eighth-rest on the fourth beat of m. 13; regard the two eighths in the anacrusis to m. 14 similarly. M. 15, note 1, lower voice, this whole-note was printed in the middle of the m. in the source.

No. 48

Allegretto—M. 26, in the source, this m. does not close at the end of the cadenza, though it appears that the normal four-beat measure has been accomplished at that time. Instead, the music proceeds into the Tempo I°. section, which then gives the measure too many beats.

No. 49

Adagio—M. 14, the notation in this m. was designed to proceed directly into the anacrusis of the Allegretto (the anacrusis accounts for the fourth beat of this measure); nowhere does Bruni account for the borrowing of the thirty-second-note which is the anacrusis to the opening Adagio.

Allegretto—M. 24, notes 1 and 2 of lower voice are eighth-notes in the source; changed here by analogy with m. 20.

No. 50

Allegretto—Anacrusis and throughout étude, *diminuendo* markings are all closed triangles (⊏══) in the source; this is the only time this type of indication is used in the source. M. 8, note 1 (double-stop) is a quarter-note in the source.

Acknowledgments

The editor wishes to thank Indiana University–Purdue University at Fort Wayne for a grant which made possible the purchase of microfilms and xerox copies from Bibliothèque nationale, Paris, and Bibliothèque du Conservatoire Royal de Musique, Brussels. Appreciation is expressed also to those libraries whose directors made available photocopies for purposes of comparison, namely, Bibliothèque nationale, Paris; Bibliothèque du Conservatoire Royale de Musique, Brussels; Bibliothèque Cantonale et Universitaire, Lausanne, Switzerland; Music Library, University of California, Berkeley; Music Library, Stanford University, Palo Alto; Music Library, The University of Iowa, Iowa City. In addition, thanks are due the Learning Resource Center, Indiana University–Purdue University at Fort Wayne, for assistance in providing the photographic plates for this edition.

January 1982

K Marie Stolba
Fort Wayne, Indiana

Notes

1. For further discussion, see K Marie Stolba, *A History of the Violin Étude to about 1800*, 2 vols. (Hays, Kansas: Fort Hays Kansas State College, 1968-69; reprint, New York: Da Capo, 1979).

2. Bruni's pedagogical works for viola, however, are rather well known.

3. "Ce musicien ne méritait pas de tomber dans l'oubli où il est maintenant plongé." François-Joseph Fétis, *Biographie universelle des musiciens et bibliographie générale de la musique (1835-44)*, 2d ed., 8 vols. (Paris: Firmin Didot Frères, fils et Cie., 1867-70), II: 99.

4. Such a chart may be found in Stolba, *A History of the Violin Étude*, I:39.

5. *Méthode pour l'alto-viola, contenant les principes de cet Instrument, suivis de Vingt-cinq Etudes, Dédiée à Monsieur Fabignon par B. Bruni*, (prix 9 f.). A Paris, chez Janet et Cotelle, Marchands de Musique ordinaires du Roi et de la Famille Royale, successeurs de M. Imbault, au Mont d'Or, rue St. Honoré, N°. 125 près celle des Poulies, et Libraires rue Neuve des Petits Champs, N°. 17, vis-à-vis le Trésor.

6. Gaetano Cesari, H. Closson, L. de la Laurencie, A. Della Corte, and C. Zino, *Antonio Bartolomeo Bruni* (Turin: S. Lattes, 1931).

7. On page 66.

8. *Mercure*, 24 March 1787, p. 192.

9. Cari Johansson, *French Music Publishers' Catalogues of the Second Half of the Eighteenth Century*, 2 vols. (Stockholm: Almquist & Wiksells, 1955), II, Facsimile No. 42.

10. Wolfgang Matthäus, *Johann André Musikverlag zu Offenbach am Main: Verlagsgeschichte und Bibliographie, 1772-1800* (Tutzing: Hans Schneider, 1973), p. 389.

11. Ibid.

12. See Johansson, *French Music Publishers' Catalogues*, I: 153. Yet Anik Devriès stated in his article "Les Éditions Musicales Sieber," in *Revue de Musicologie* 55 (1969): 22, that Jean-Georges Sieber had ". . . cessé toute publicité dans les périodiques française de 1799 à 1812. . . ."

13. Matthäus, *Johann André*, p. 389.

14. Ibid.

15. Though this publication shows No. 85 as address of Sieber *père*, the facsimile of the catalog given by Johansson shows "Rue St. Honoré entre la Rue des Vielles Etuves et celle d'Orleans chez Apottacaire N°. 92" (Johansson, *French Music Publishers' Catalogues*, II, Facsimile No. 117). Actually, both numbers may indicate the identical location, for during the period between 1795 and 1809 there were many changes in names and numbers of Parisian streets. See also Devriès, "Les Éditions," p. 41.

16. The copy of this 2me *Partie* which is among the holdings of the Music Library, University of Iowa, Iowa City, is conjecturally dated "[ca. 1795]," which, in the light of the above findings, would seem to be a few years too early.

17. The formality of this address, with the absence of Pignatelli's given name, and the reference to His Majesty Charles, King of Spain, without identification by Roman numeral, makes it difficult to identify which Pignatelli received the dedicatory honor. Undoubtedly it was one of two princes of

Strongoli who bore the name Francesco. Both were military men. The elder Francesco (1734-1812) reportedly was entrusted with handling some rather delicate negotiations with Charles III of Spain for Italian royalty. While there is no mention of association with Spanish royalty in connection with the younger Francesco (1775-1853), nephew of the former, it is known that he achieved the military rank of Brigadier-General. For further information, consult Moscati Ruggero, *Enciclopedia italiana di scienze, lettere ed arti* (Rome: Istituto della Enciclopedia italiana, 1935-45), 27: 269-70.

18. While Lionel de la Laurencie recognized the existence of both the *Caprices & Airs variés en forme d'étude pour un violon seul* and *Cinquante Études pour le violon formant la seconde partie,* as he referred to the second volume, he apparently was not aware of the existence of the other volume bearing the title *Cinquante Études*. In his discussion of Bruni's pedagogical violin compositions La Laurencie indicates that Bruni composed only two collections of études for the violin (Cesari, Closson, de la Laurencie, Della Corte, and Zino, *Antonio Bartolomeo Bruni,* p. 181), that the *Cinquante Études* form a second part to the *Caprices & Airs variés,* and that Andreas Moser was misinformed when he indicated that Bruni composed "*200 études pour le violon (publiées en deux séries), . . .*" (Ibid.). What Andreas Moser actually wrote in *Die Violine und ihre Meister* concerning Bruni was: ". . . *er hat neben 100 Etuden für die Violine (sie wurden in zwei Serien publiziert), . . .*" (Moser, p. 96). Apparently, Moser had examined both volumes entitled *Cinquante Études*, though he seems not to have been aware of the *Caprices & Airs variés en forme d'étude.*

19. *Répertoire Internationale des Sources Musicales,* ed. Karl-Heinz Schlager, I: 439, B 4810.

20. Stolba, *A History of the Violin Étude,* I:8.

21. The violin bow attained its present form through the successful experiments of François Tourte (1747-1835) in the 1780s; it is probable that Bruni had at his disposal one of the earliest of the "modern" violin bows. The violin underwent many structural adjustments during the eighteenth century; by 1787 most of these had already been made, though neck and fingerboard continued to be lengthened until shortly after 1800. Still lacking, though, was the chin rest, which Ludwig Spohr claimed in 1832 that he had invented ten years previously. For further information, consult Stolba, *A History of the Violin Étude,* I: 25-37; David D. Boyden, "The Violin and its Technique in the 18th Century," *The Musical Quarterly* XXXVI (January 1950); Edward Heron-Allen, *Violin-Making, As It Was and Is* (London: Ward, Lock & Co., 1885).

22. Examples cited are representative; others may be located within the volume.

23. Leopold Mozart, *A Treatise on the Fundamental Principles of Violin Playing* (1756), trans. Editha Knocker, 2d ed. (London: Oxford University Press, 1951), p. 188.

24. Ibid., p. 166.

25. Giuseppe Tartini, *Traité des Agréments de la Musique,* ed. Erwin R. Jacobi (Celle: Moeck, 1961), p. 65.

26. Mozart, *A Treatise,* p. 171.

27. Ibid., p. 167. See also Tartini, *Traité,* p. 66.

28. Tartini, *Traité,* p. 66.

29. Johann Joachim Quantz, *Versuch einer Anweisung die Flöte traversière zu spielen* (1752), trans. and with commentary by Edward Randolph Reilly, published as *On Playing the Flute* (London: Faber and Faber, 1966), p. 228.

30. Tartini, *Traité,* p. 69.

31. Ibid.

32. Mozart, *A Treatise,* p. 171.

33. Ibid., p. 45.

34. Ibid. Quantz also discussed these bowing strokes and differentiated them by saying that notes with wedges "must be cut short, but those with dots, merely made with a short bow-stroke, and held on." (Quantz, *Versuch,* XVII: ii, p. 5.)

35. Boyden, "The Violin," p. 367; Quantz, *Versuch,* p. 217.

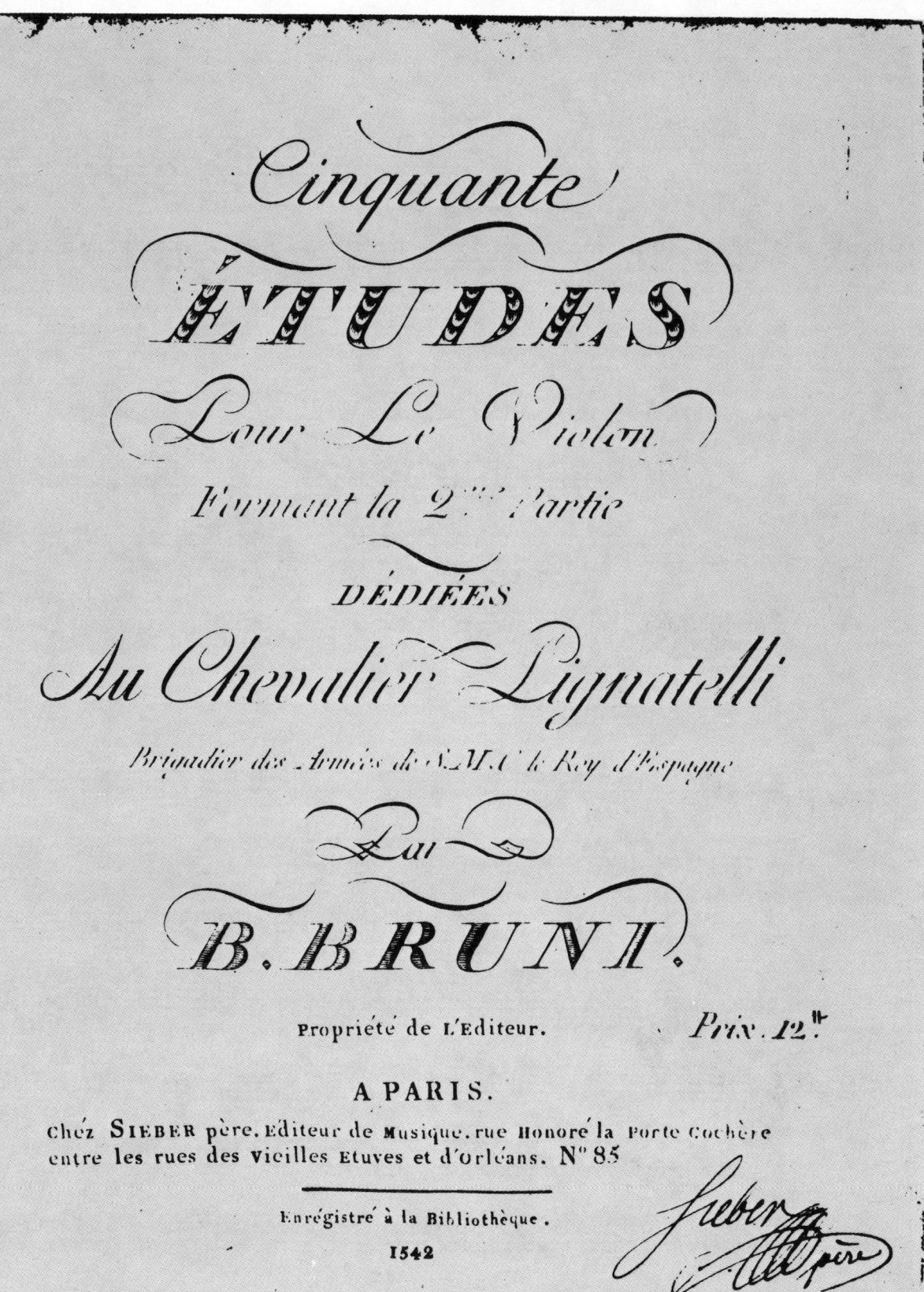

Plate I. A. B. Bruni, *Cinquante Études*, title page.

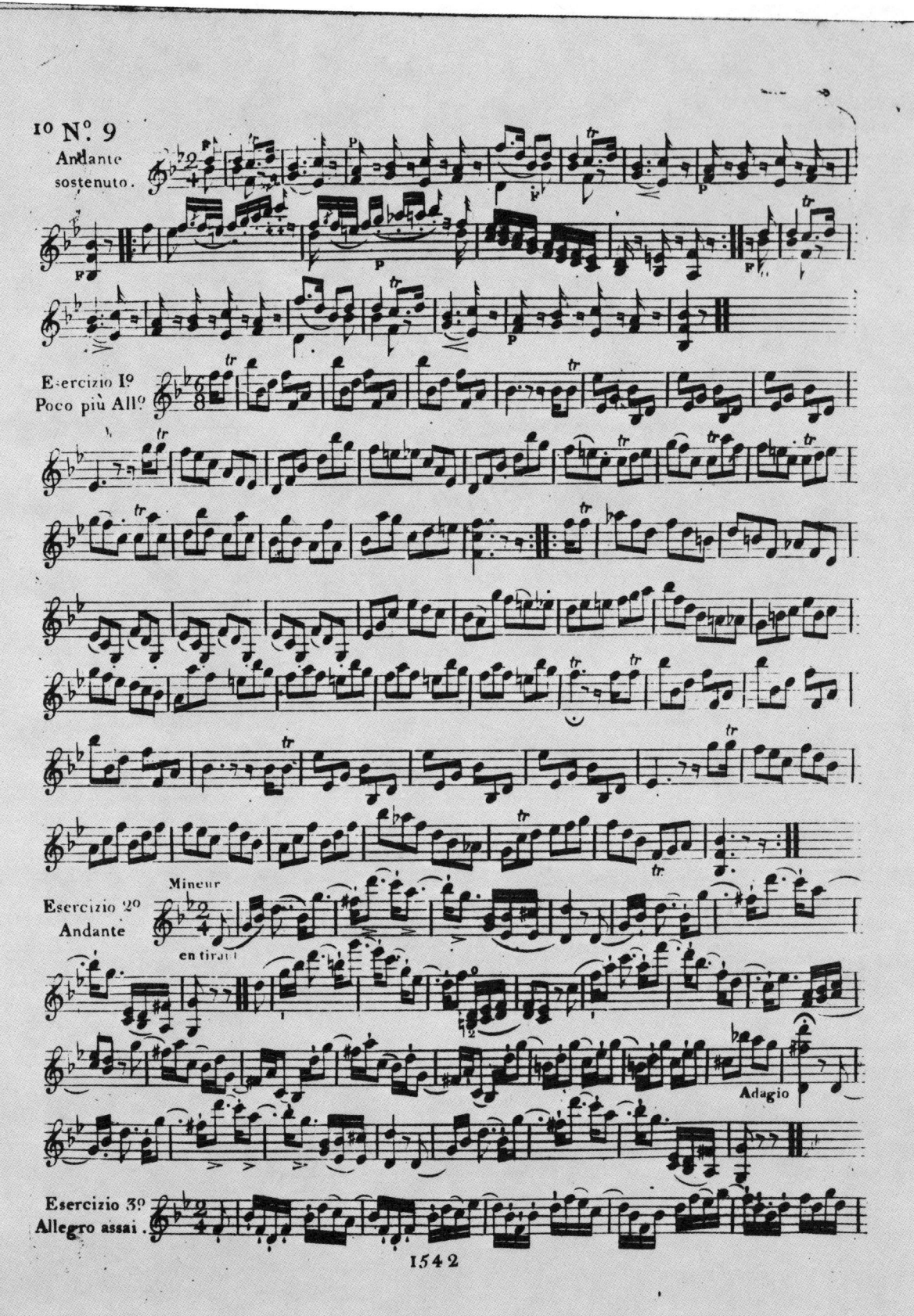

Plate II. A. B. Bruni, *Cinquante Études*, p. 10.

CAPRICES & AIRS VARIÉS EN FORME D'ÉTUDE POUR UN VIOLON SEUL

No. 1

No. 2

No. 3
Andante

No. 4
Allegro

No. 5

No. 6

No. 13

No. 14

No. 15

No. 16

No. 17

No. 19

No. 20

No. 21

No. 22

Aria con Variationi. Andante

No. 23

No. 24

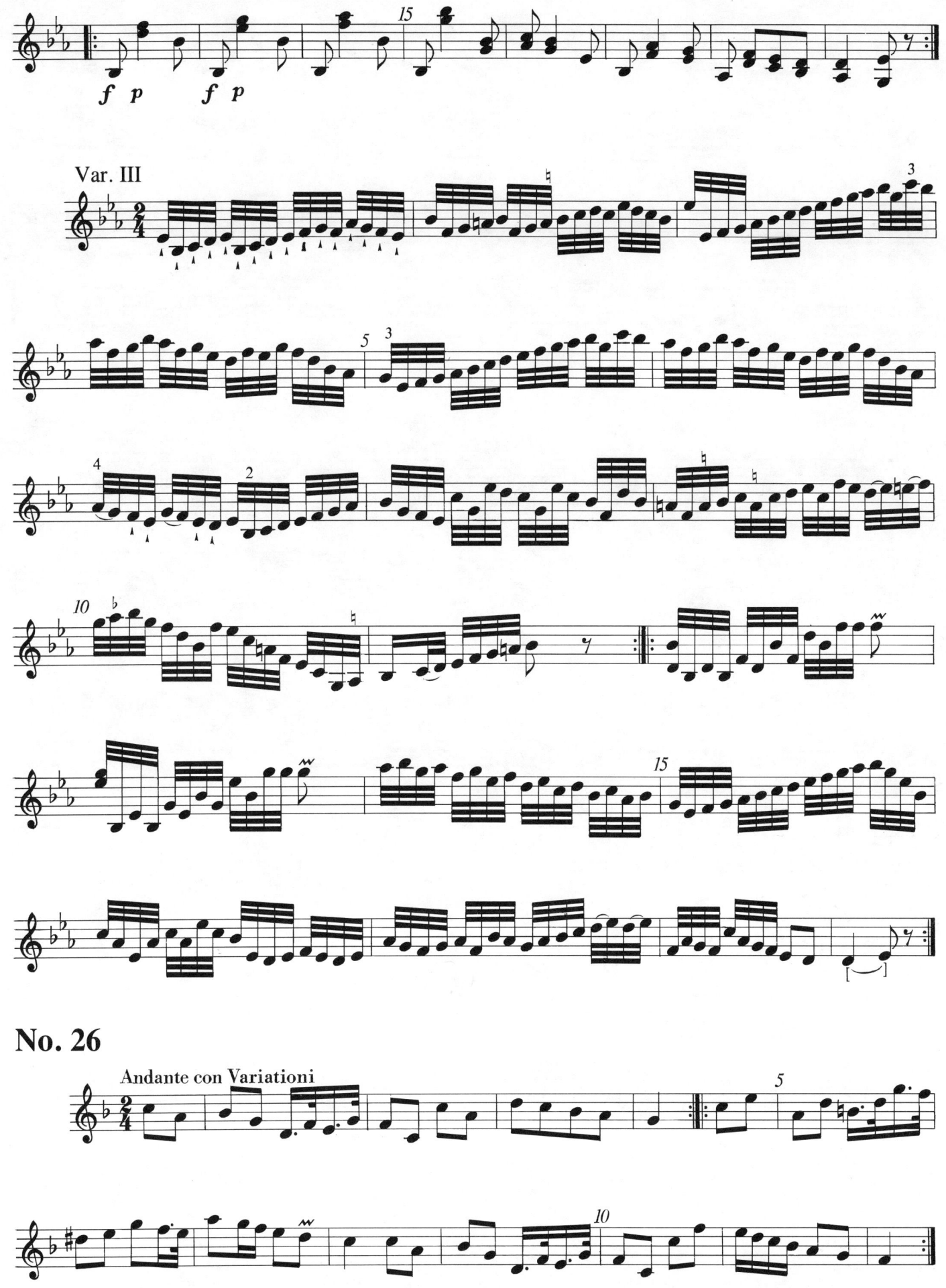

No. 27

Var. III

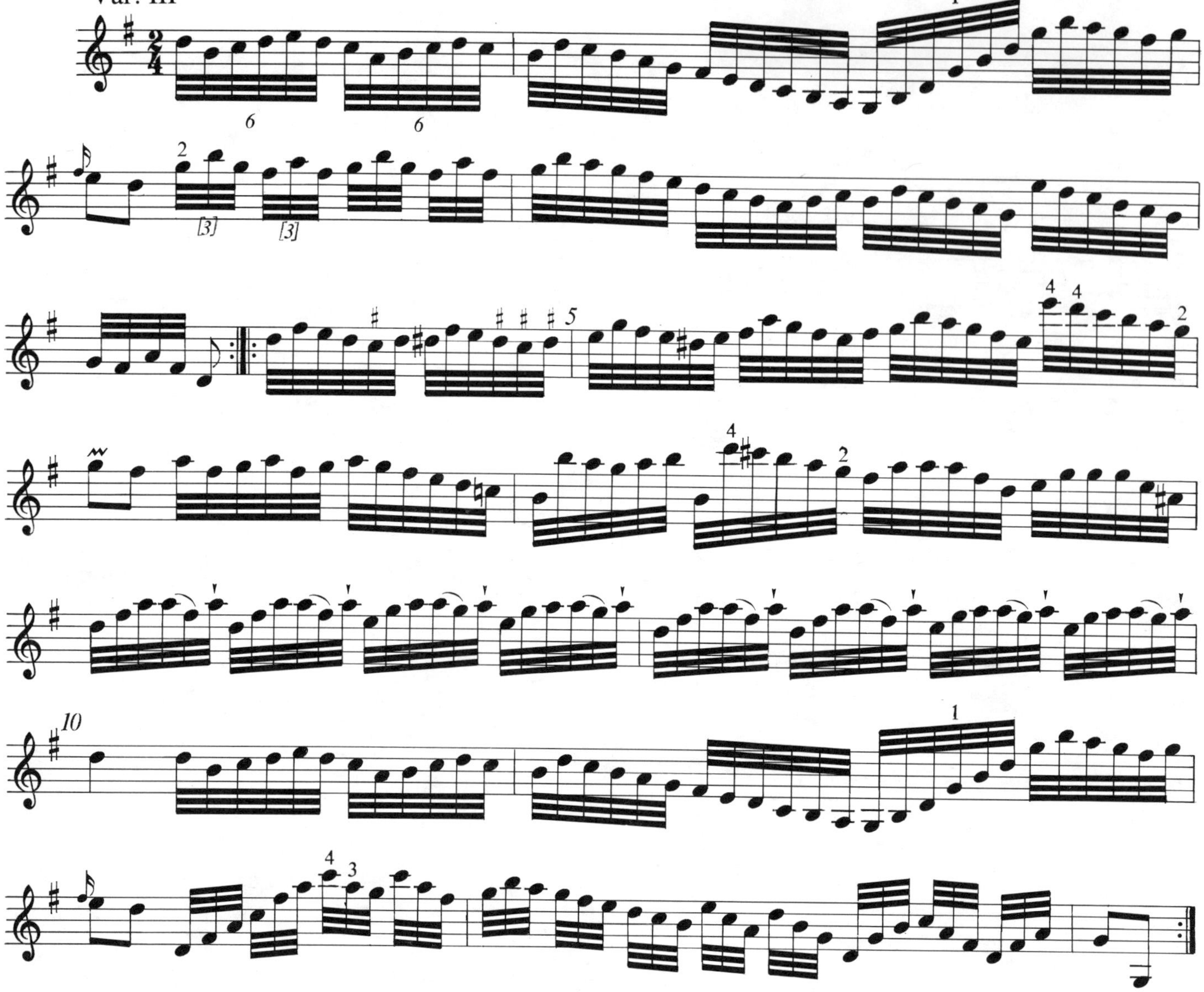

No. 28

Andante con Variationi

Var. I

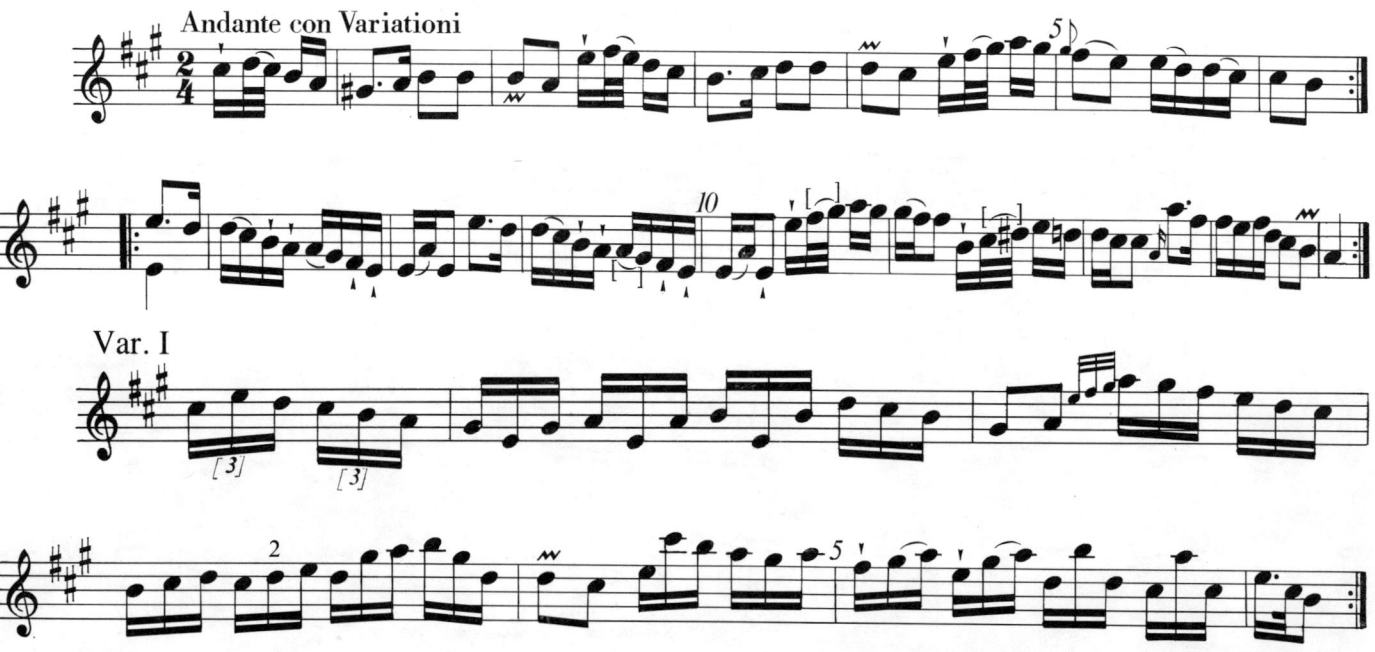

No. 29

CINQUANTE ÉTUDES POUR LE VIOLON FORMANT LA 2.ᵐᵉ PARTIE

No. 1

No. 2

No. 4

No. 5

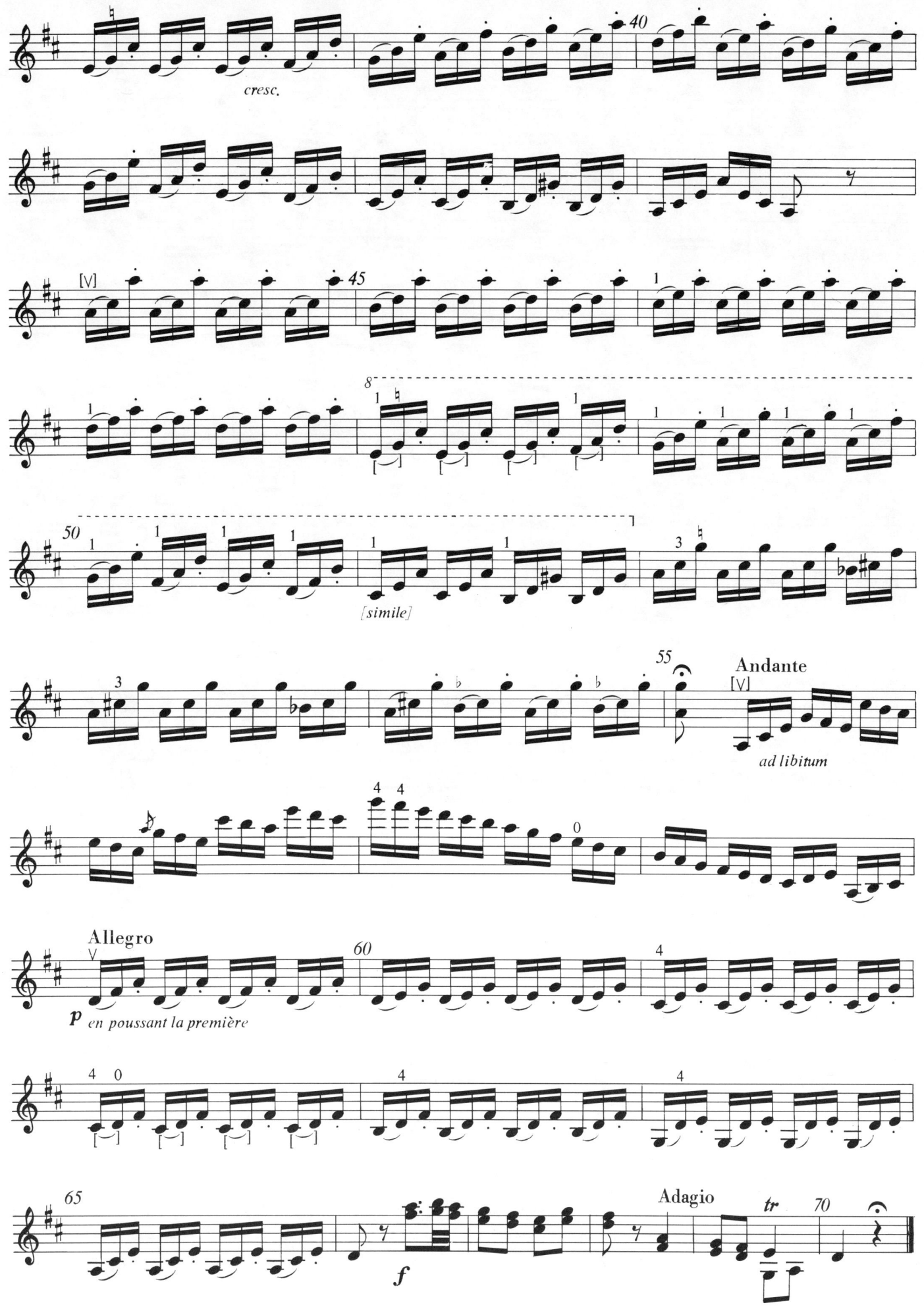

No. 6

Tempo di Minuetto. Allegro

Mineur

Minuetto D.C.

No. 7

Aria. Andante sostenuto

No. 9

Esercizio 1º

Minuetto D.C.

Esercizio 2º

Mineur. Andante

Esercizio 3º
Allegro assai

No. 10

Polonaise

Majeur. Minuetto Italiano
Poco più Andante

[Fine]

Polonaise D.C.

No. 11

No. 12

No. 13

No. 14

No. 15

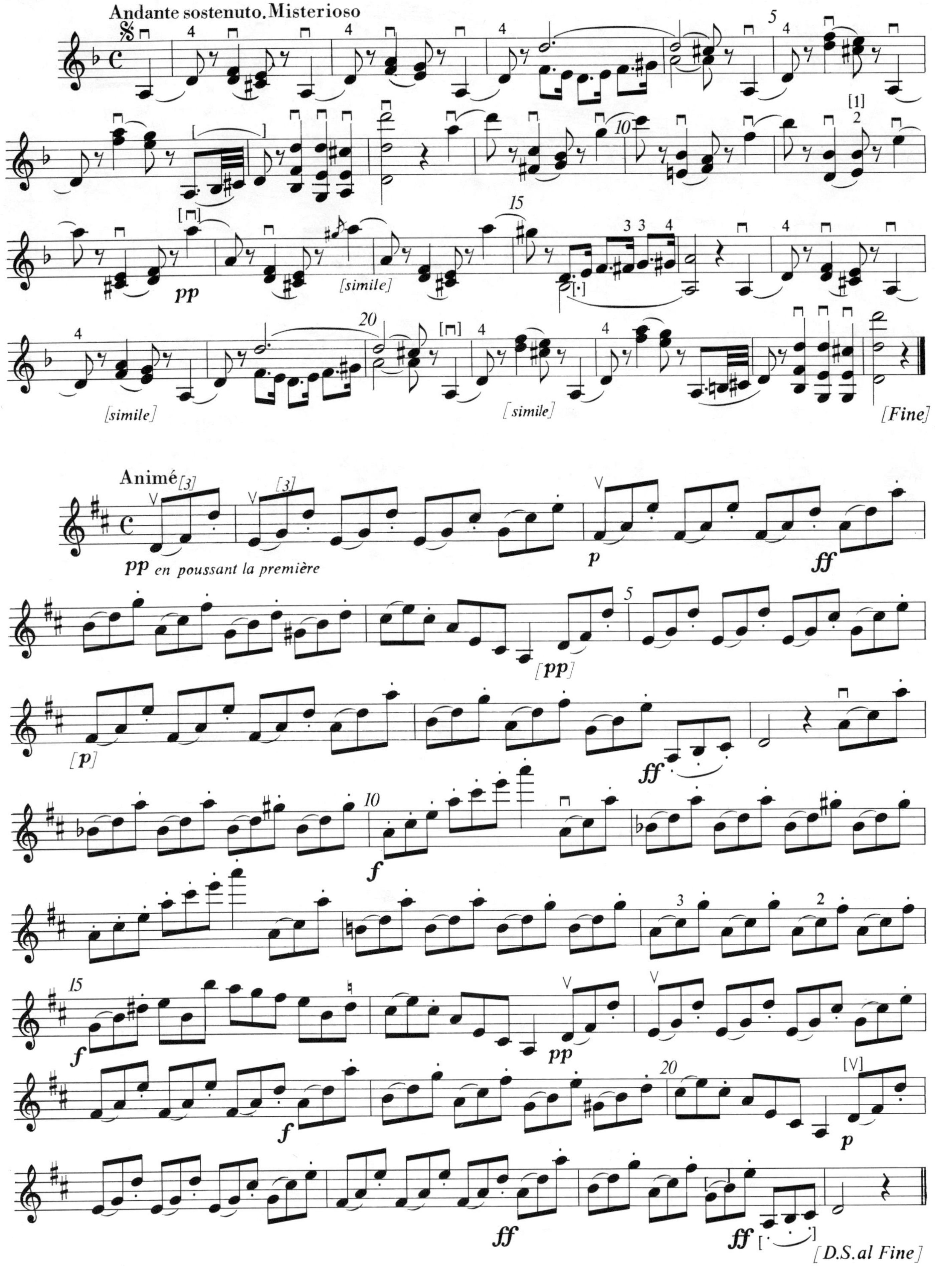
Andante sostenuto, Misterioso
pp
[simile]
[simile]
[simile]
[Fine]
Animé
pp en poussant la première
p
ff
[pp]
[p]
ff
f
f
pp
f
p
ff
ff
[D.S. al Fine]

No. 16

Esercizio

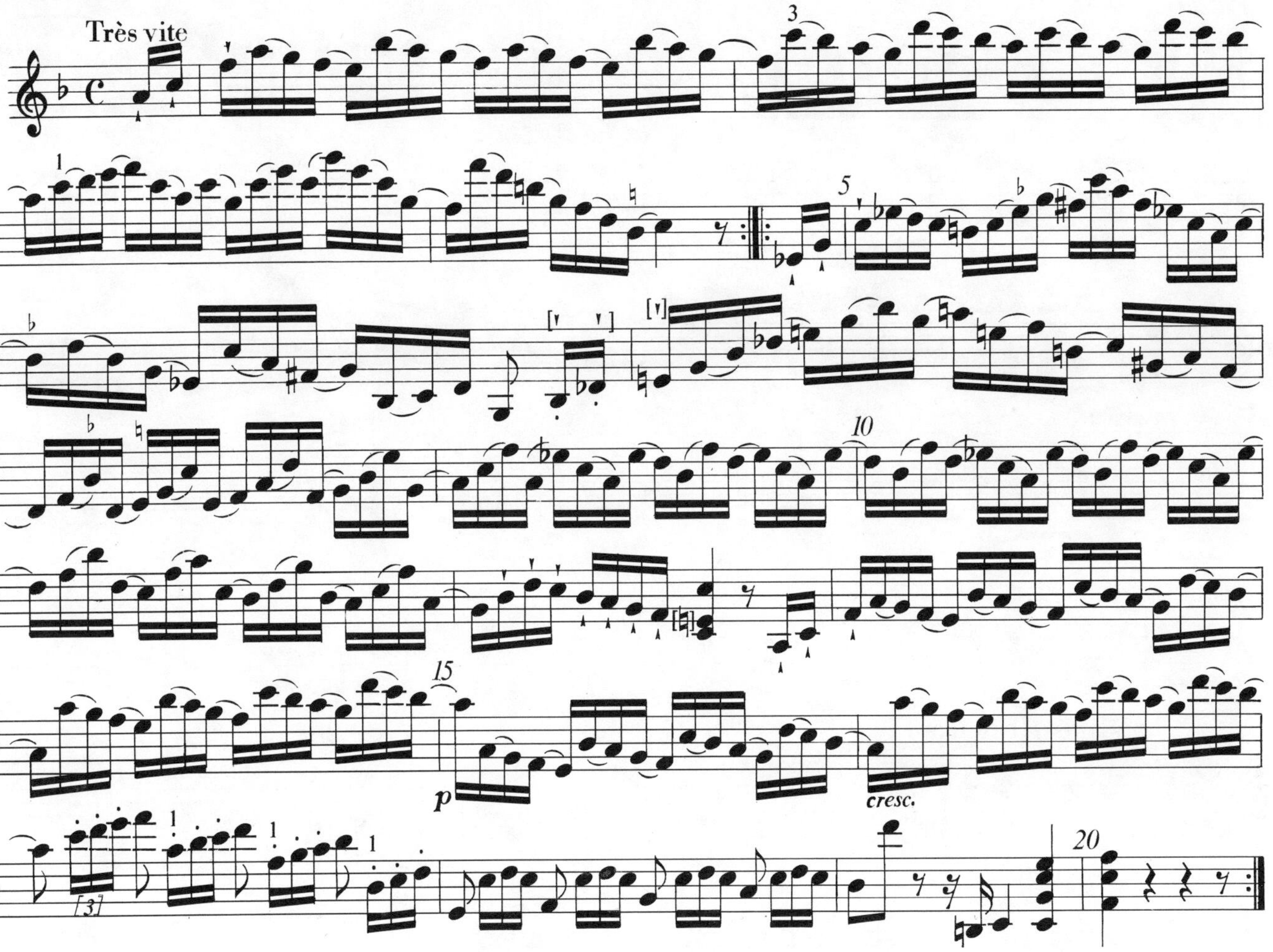

Très vite

No. 17

Tempo di Minuetto

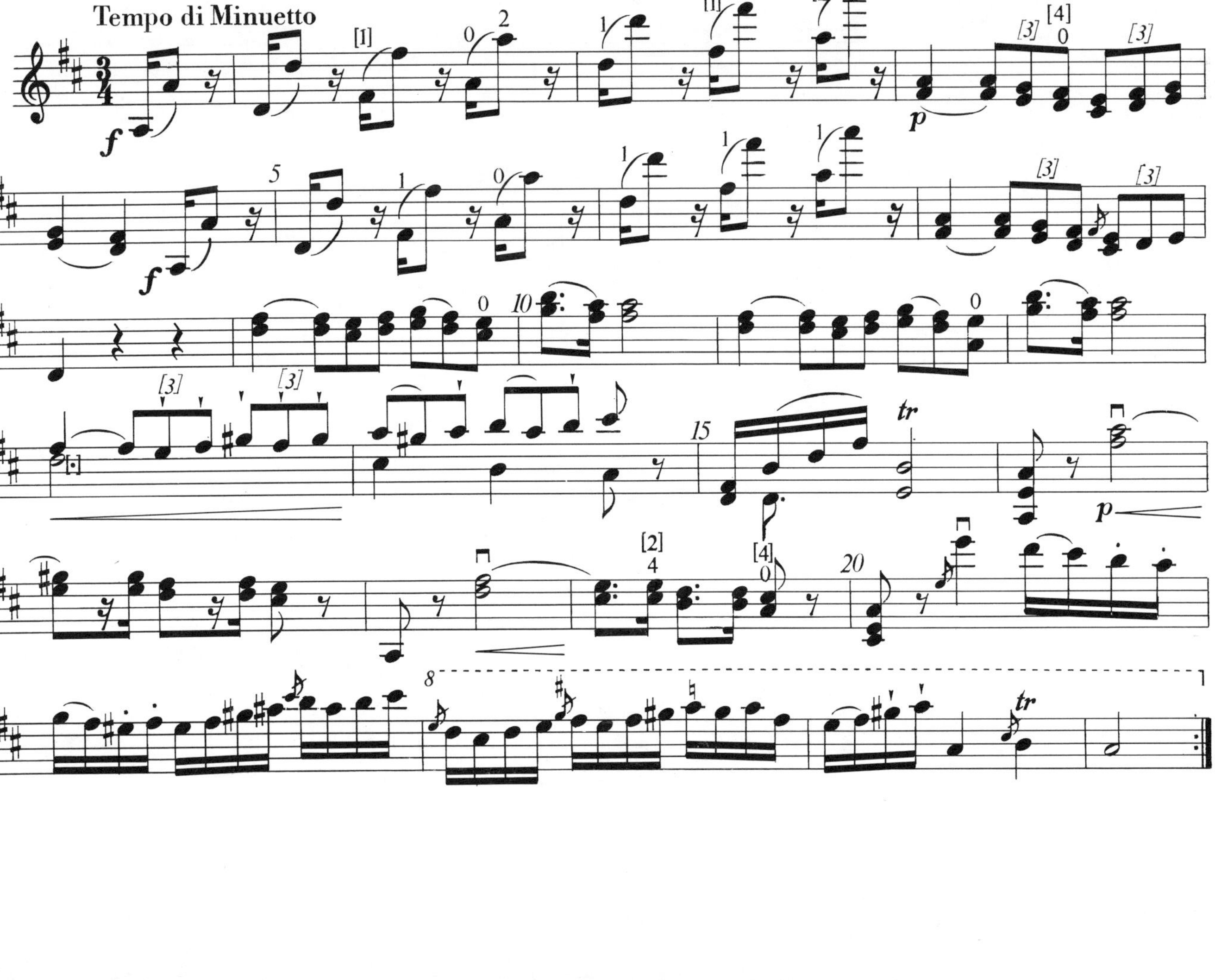

No. 19

No. 20

D.C.[D.S. al Fine]

No. 21

No. 22

Tempo di Menuetto. Sostenuto

Adagio
Tempo I

No. 23

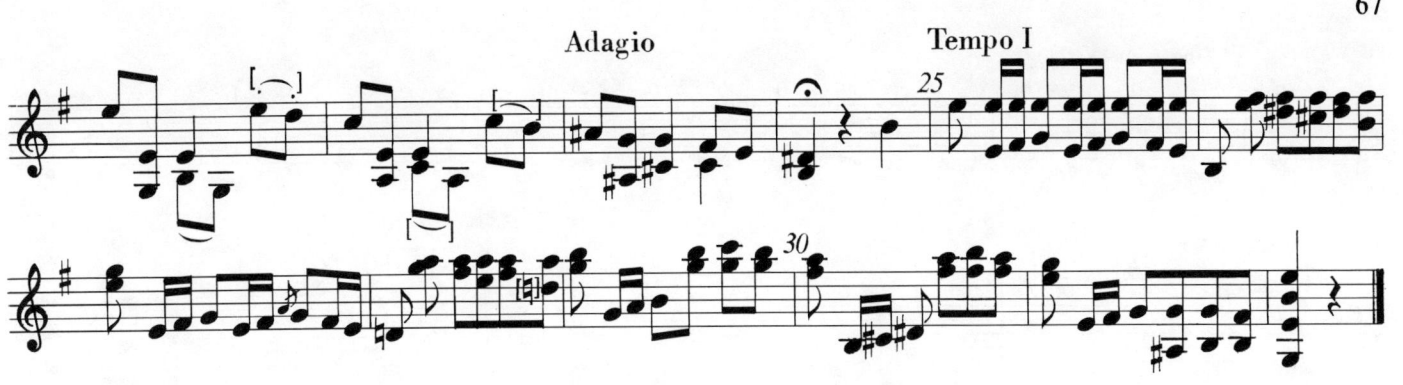

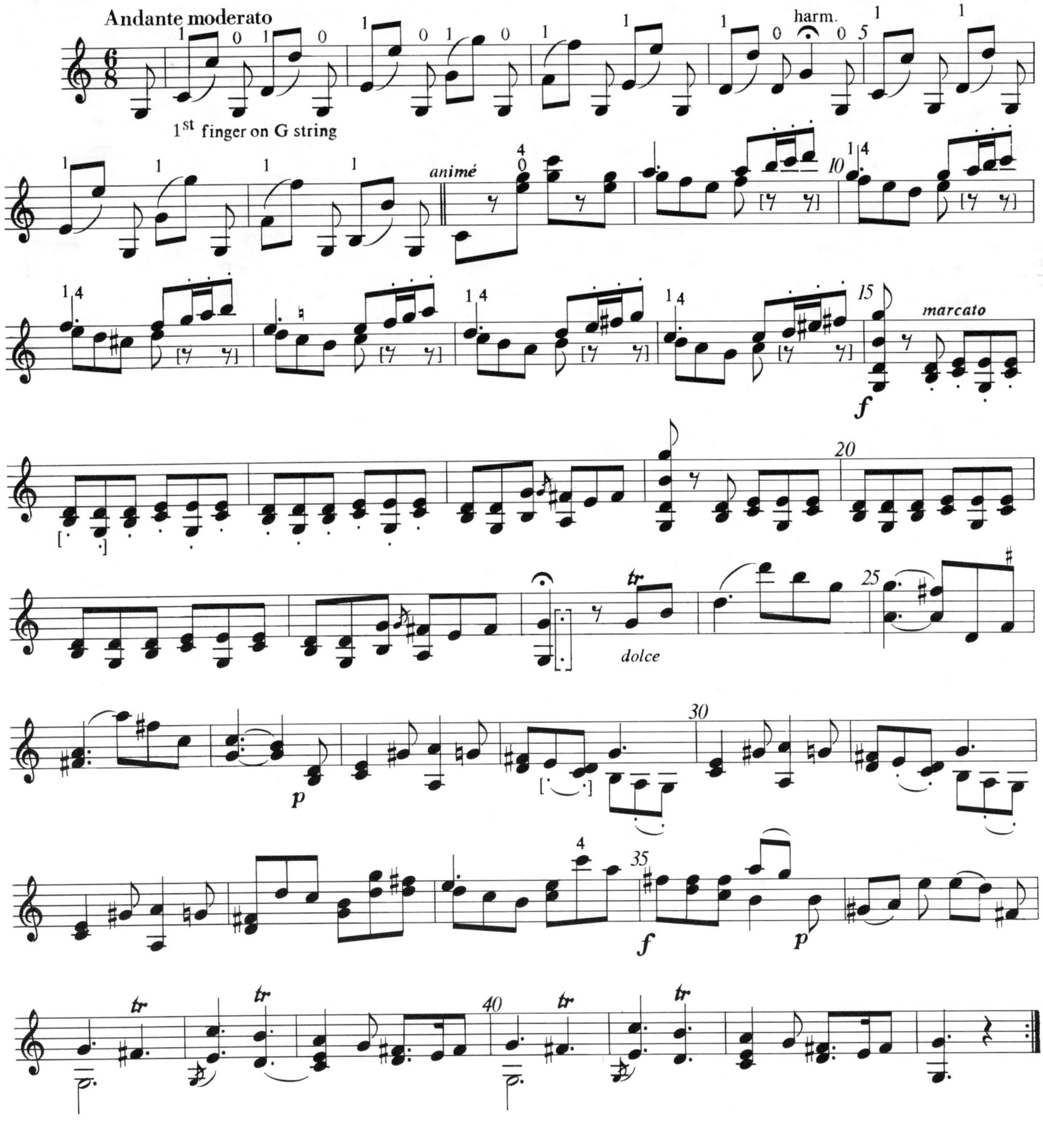
Andante moderato
1st finger on G string
harm.
animé
marcato
dolce

No. 24 Moderato.Con Brio

No. 25

No. 26

No. 27

Pastorale. Andante
p
tr
Fine

Mineur. Allegro
staccato
f
p
[simile]

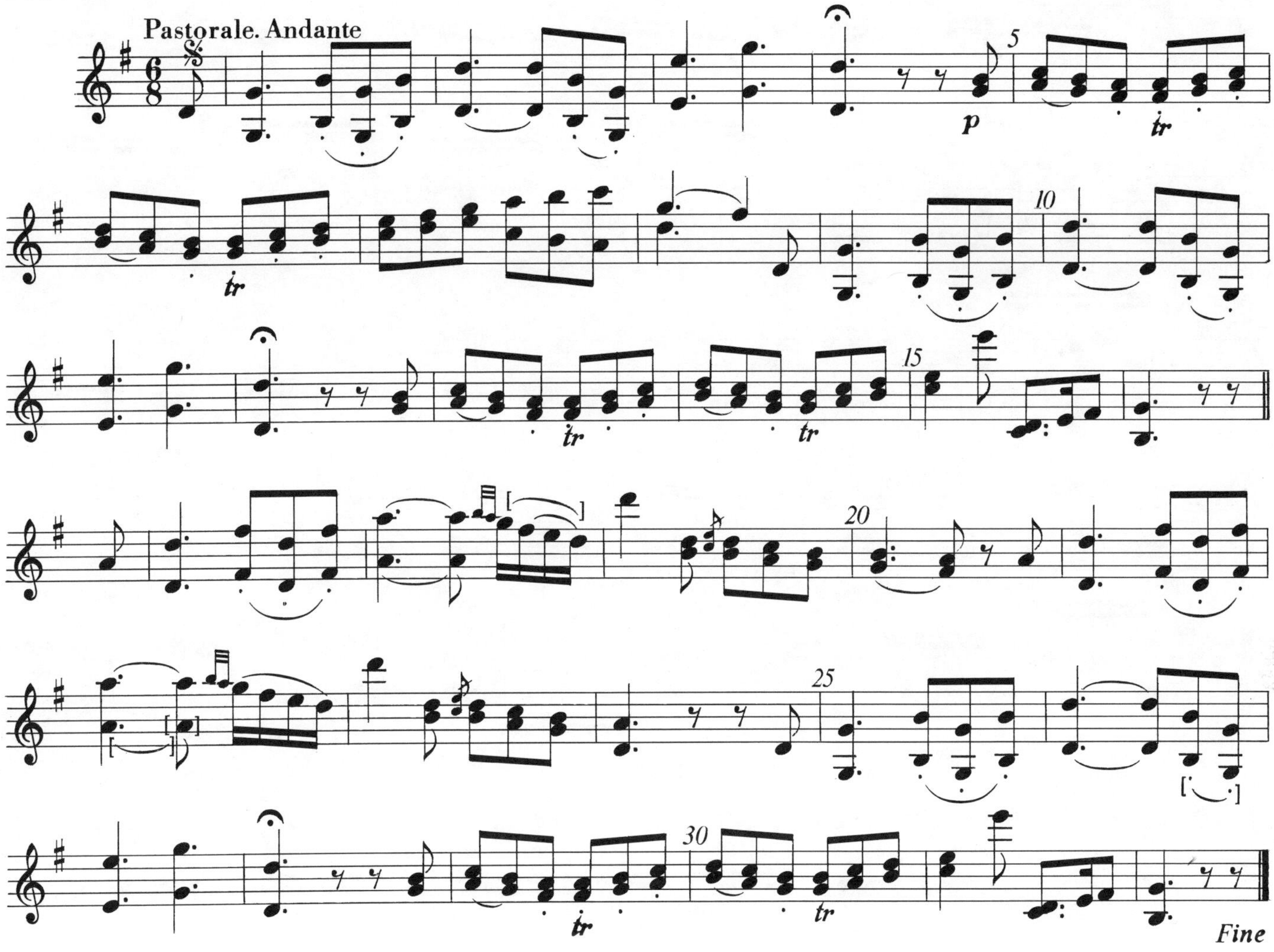

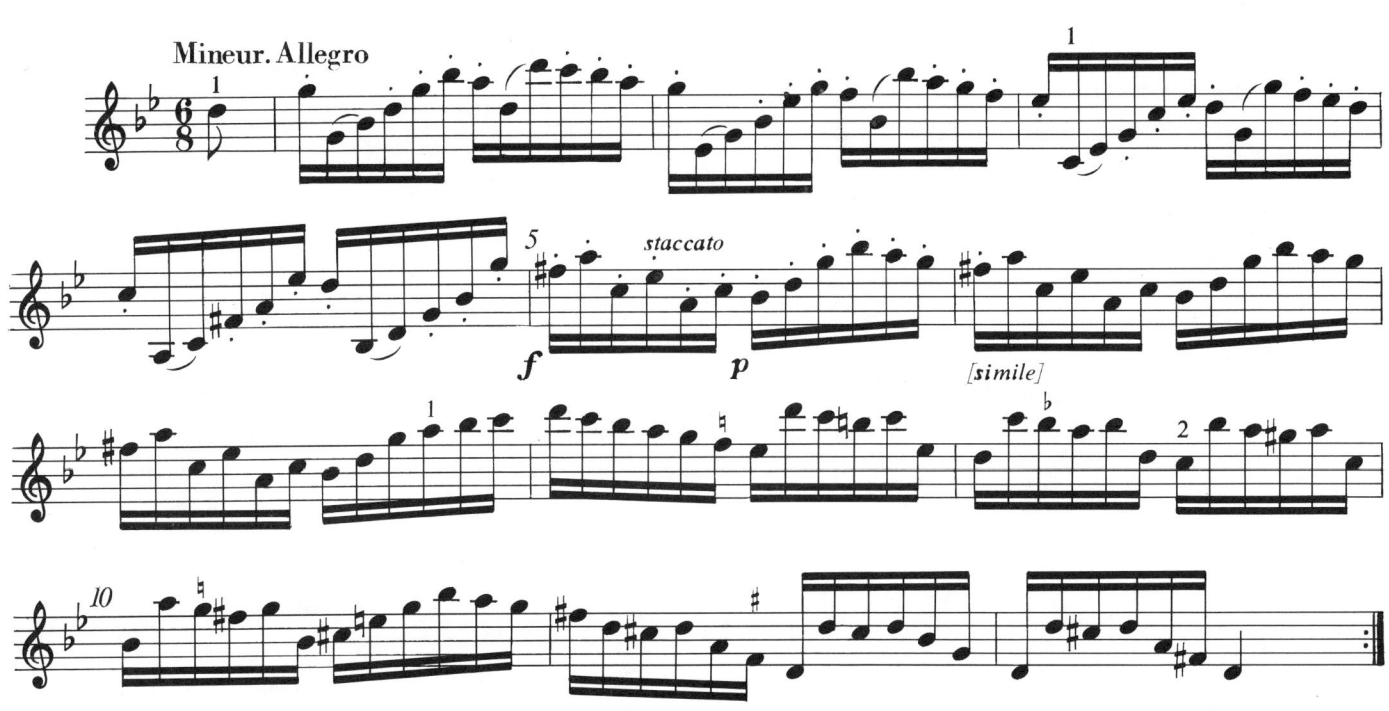

No. 28

Tempo di Minuetto. Quasi Adagio

Esercizio 4º
Majeur. Più Andante

Esercizio 5º
Primo Tempo

No. 29
Andante sostenuto

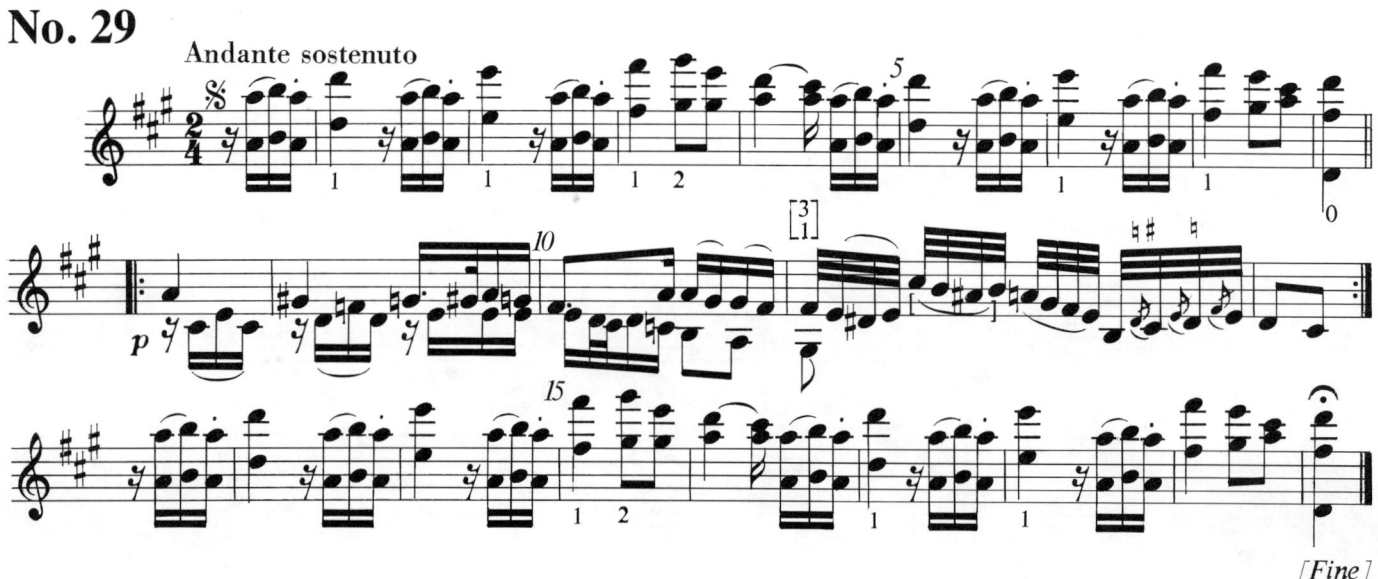

[Fine]

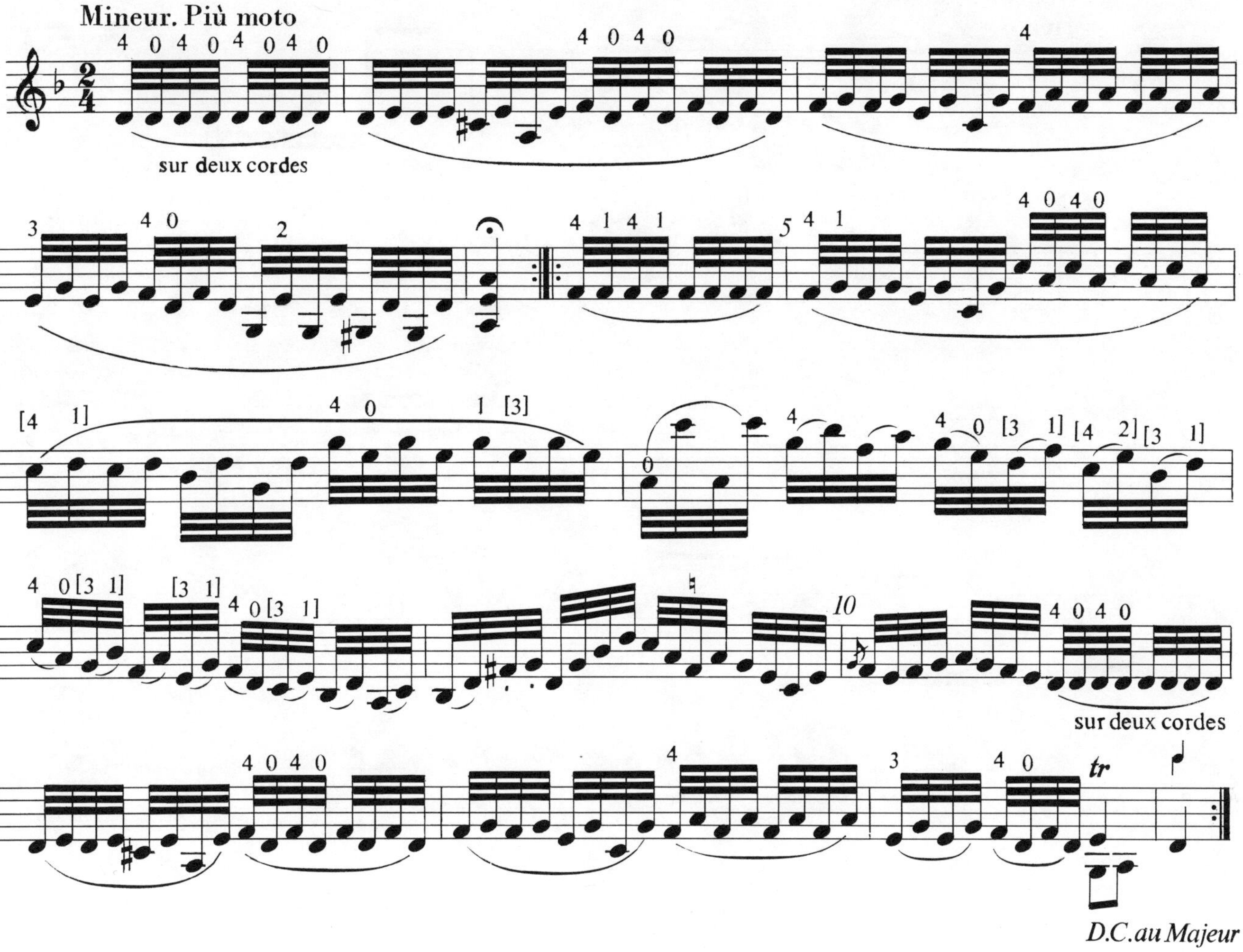
Mineur. Più moto
sur deux cordes
sur deux cordes
D.C. au Majeur

No. 30

Siciliana. Andantino
[simile]
Fine

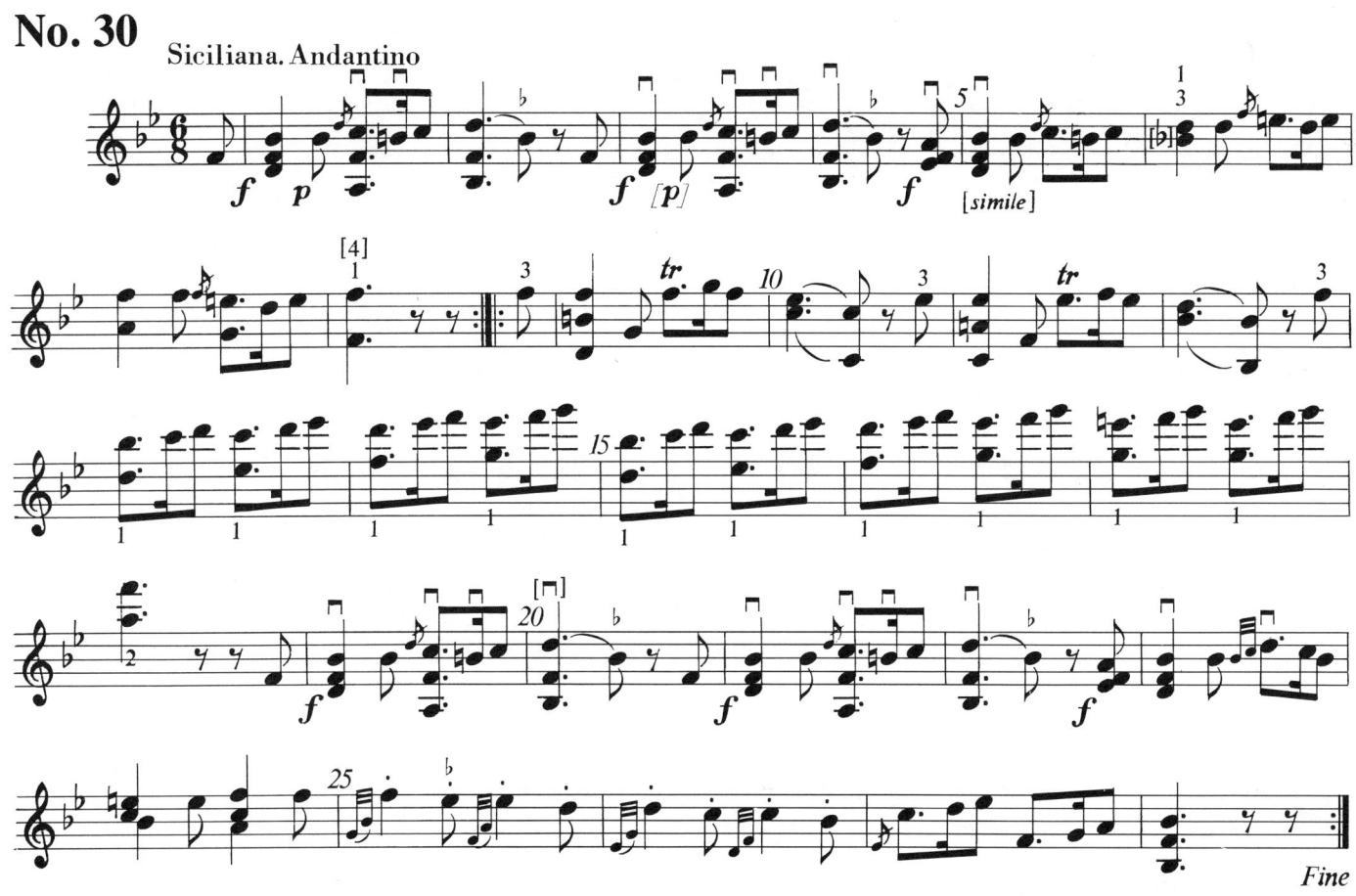

Mineur

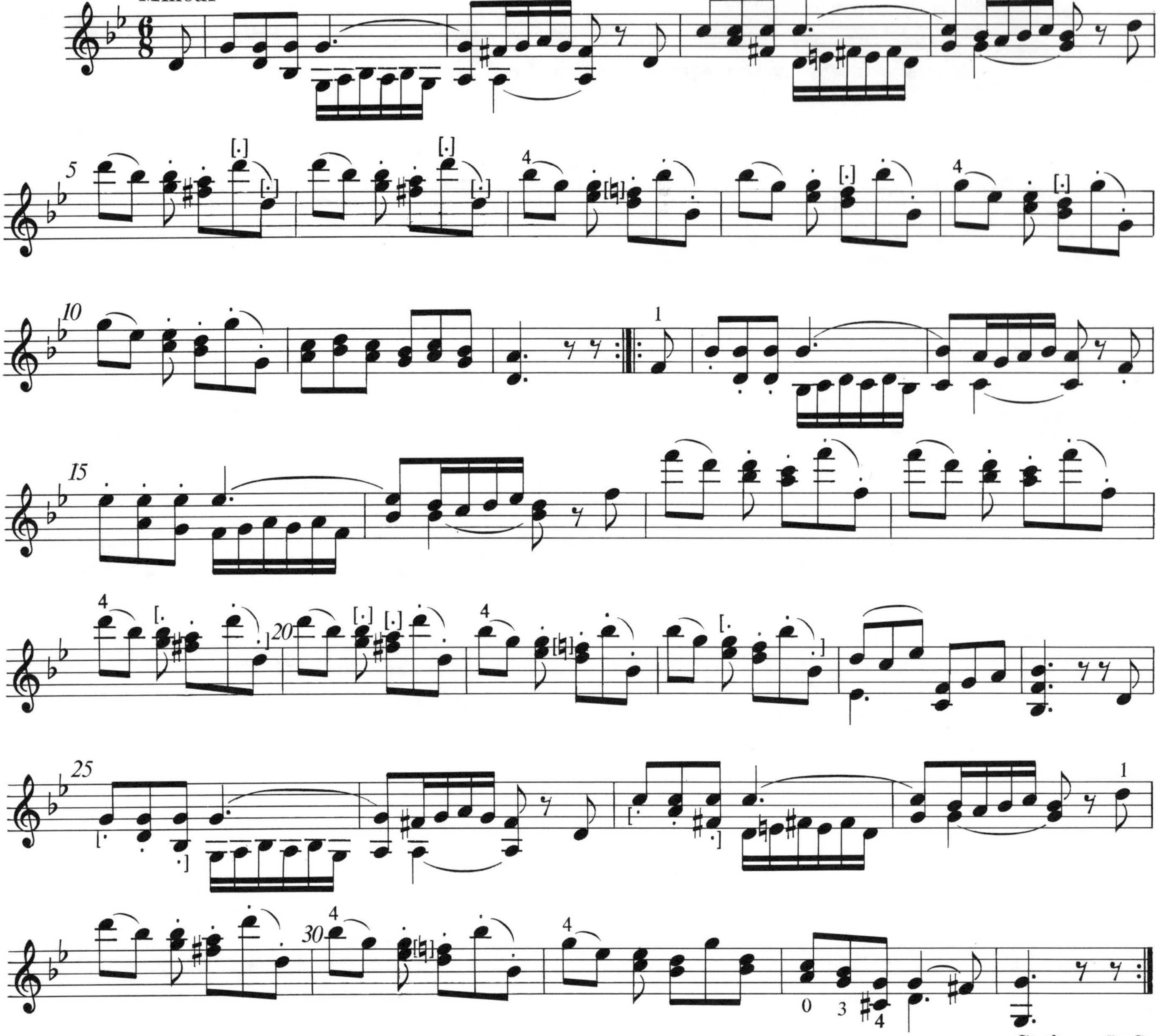

Siciliana D.C.

No. 31

Tempo di Minuetto

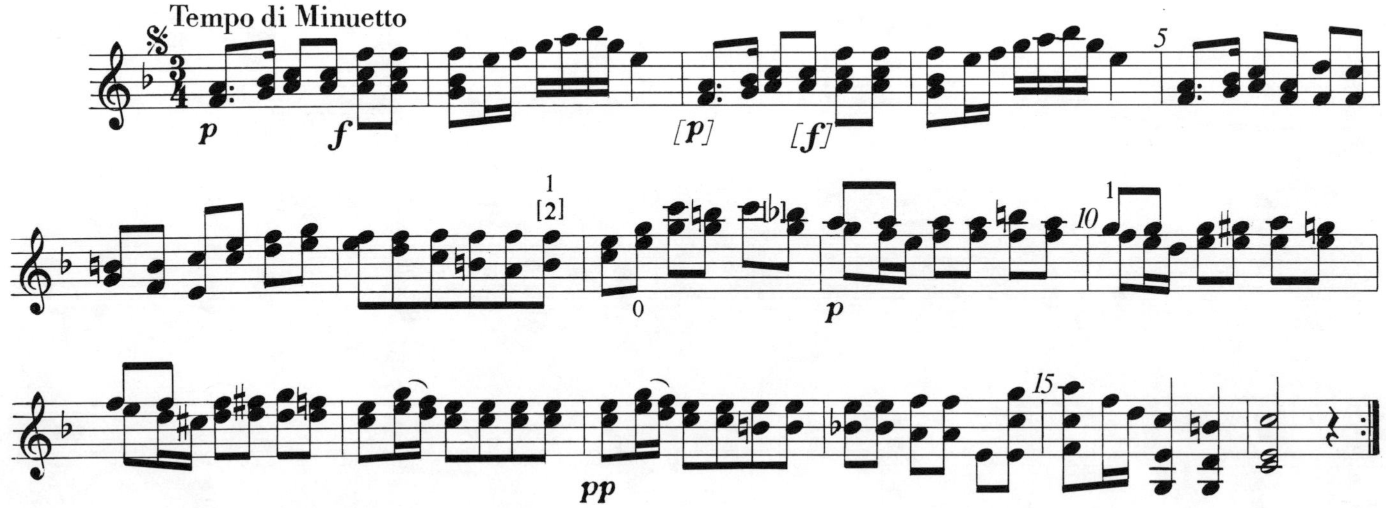

80

[Minuetto D.C.]

No. 32

Aria. Quasi Adagio

No. 34

D.C. au Majeur

No. 35

Andante con moto

Esercizio 1.mo

Andante Sostenuto

Esercizio 2º
Allegretto

No. 37 Adagio

No. 38

Aria. Adagio

2ᵉ corde

[Fine]

Esercizio 1º

Allegro

Esercizio 2º
Allegro moderato

Esercizio 3º
Andante

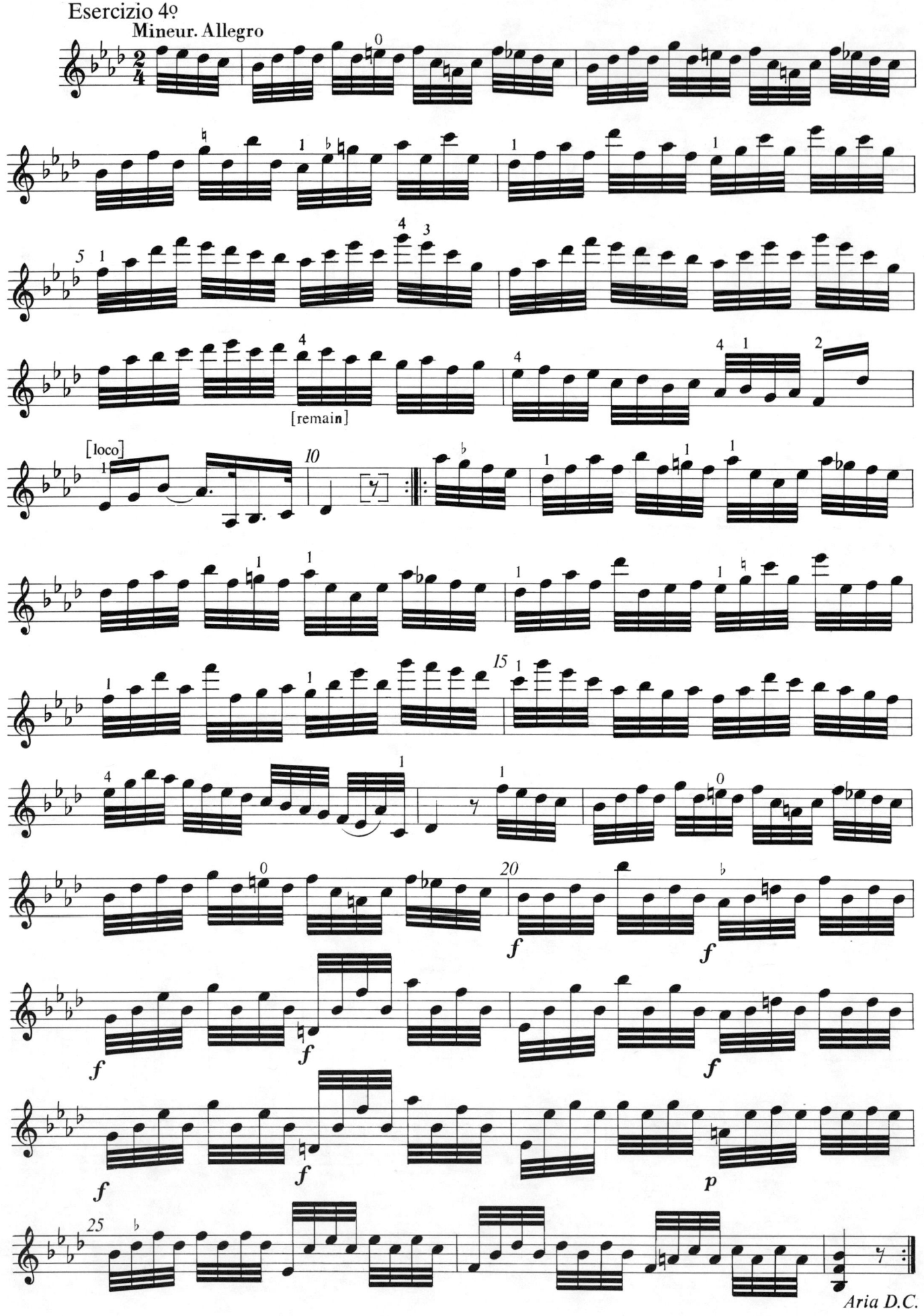

No. 39

No. 40

No. 41
Esercizio

No. 42

Andante sostenuto

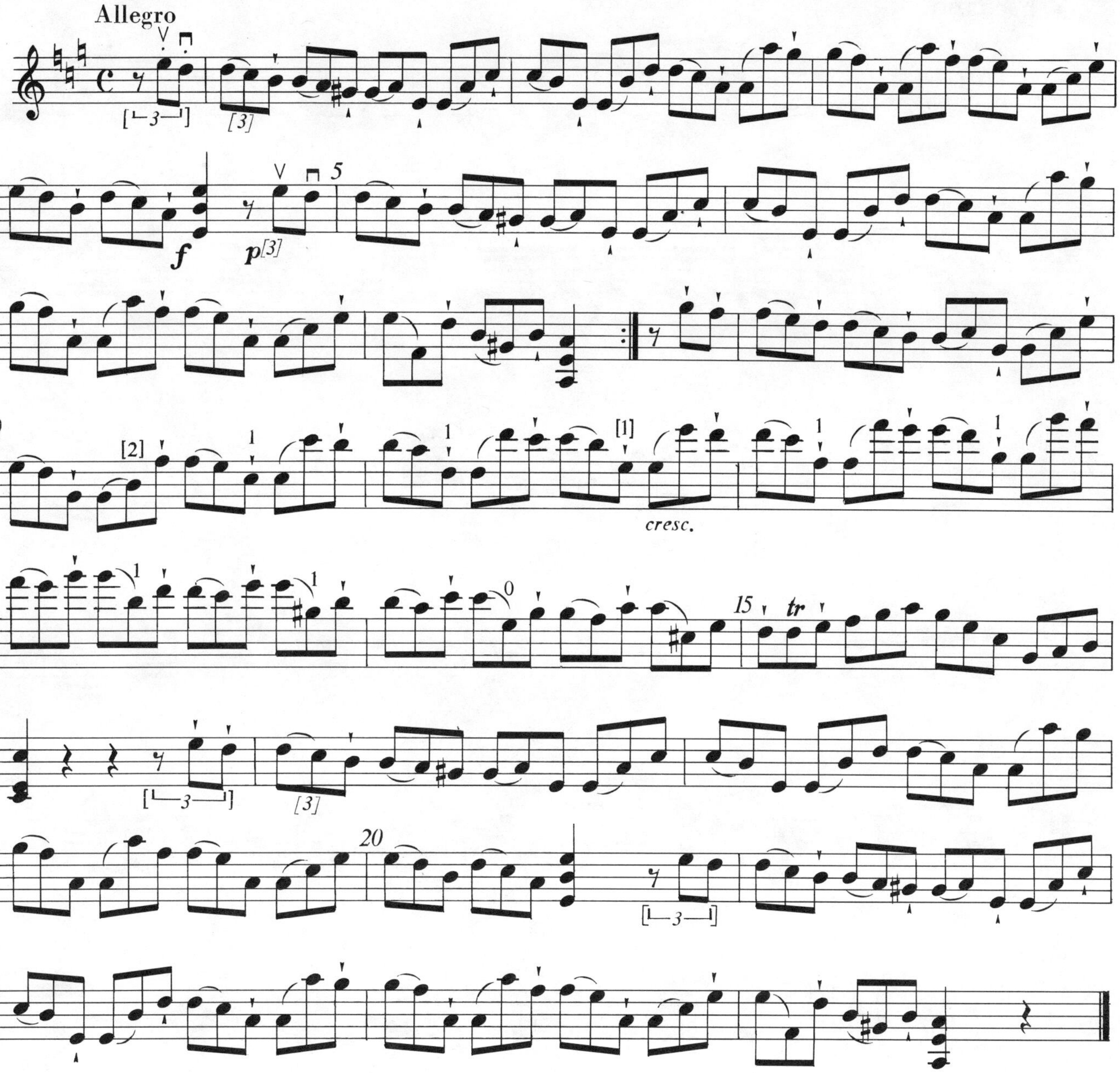
Allegro
f
p
cresc.
tr

Moderato
f
p

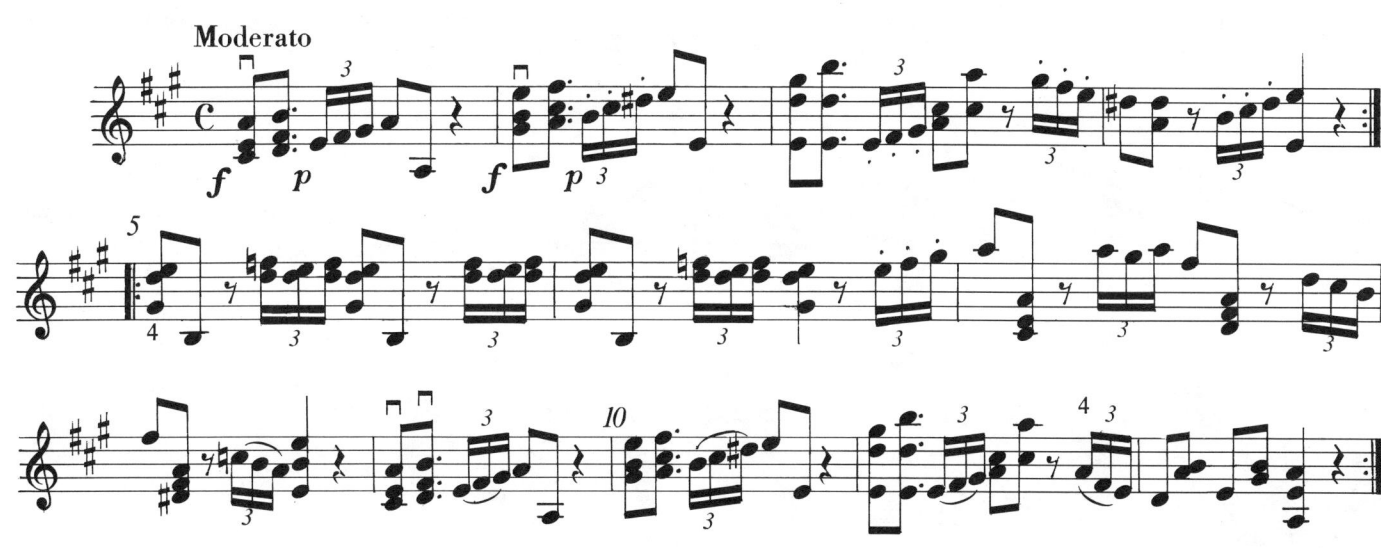

104

Esercizio

No. 44

No. 45

Mineur D.C.

No. 46

Grazioso

Diminuez le mouvement.

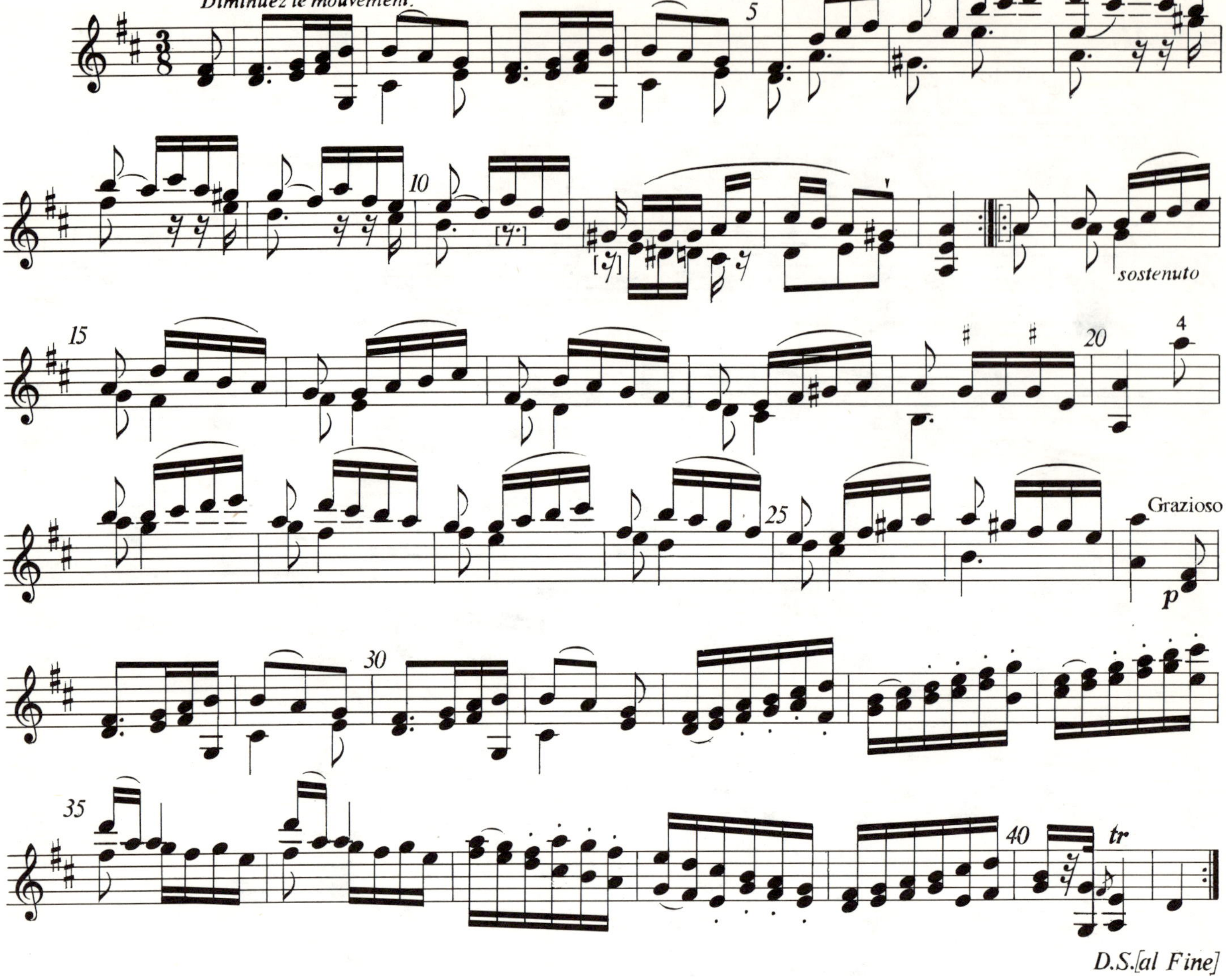

No. 47 Moderato

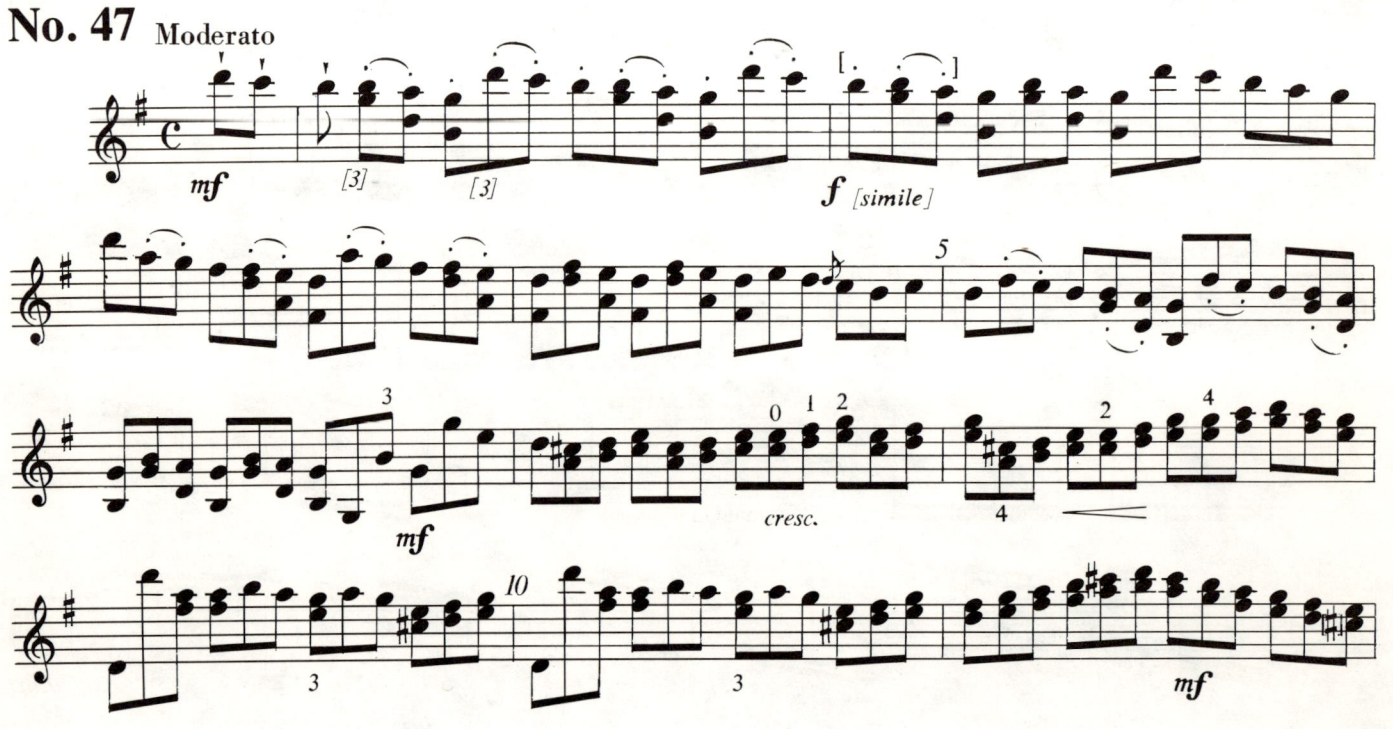

No. 48

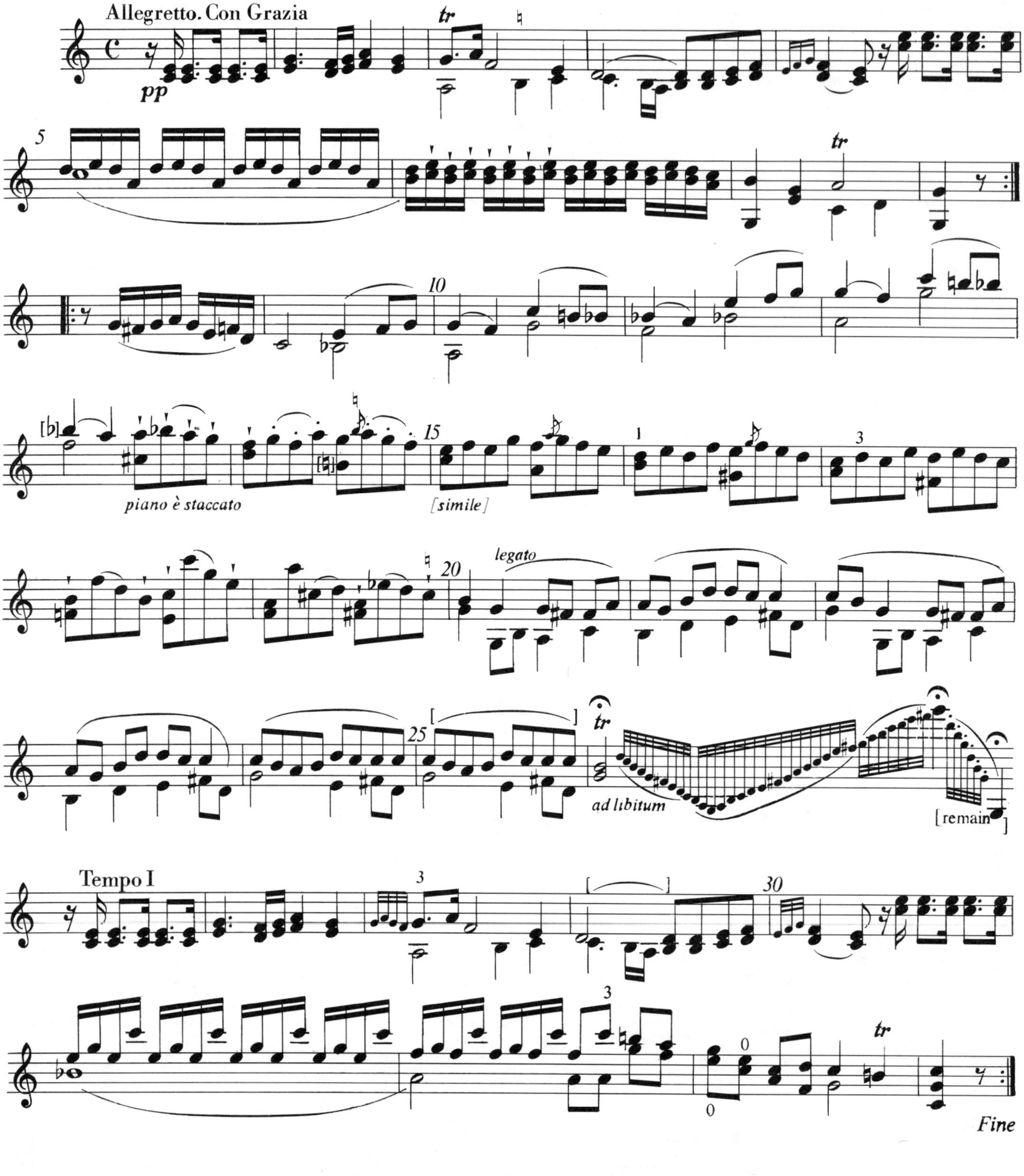
Allegretto. Con Grazia
pp
tr
5
tr
10
piano è staccato
15
[simile]
legato
20
25
tr
ad libitum
[remain]
Tempo I
30
tr
Fine

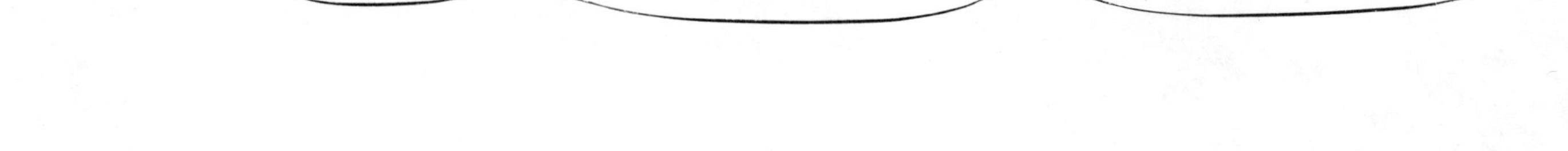
Mineur

115

Majeur D.C.

No. 49

[Fine]

Mineur

[simile]

Majeur [Allegretto] D.C.

118

No. 50